KU-259-889

500 Miles of Gratitude

My Journey on the Camino de Santiago

James R. McInnis

WESTBOW
PRESS®
A DIVISION OF THOMAS NELSON
& ZONDERVAN

WestBow Press books may be ordered through booksellers or by contacting:

WestBow Press
A Division of Thomas Nelson & Zondervan
1663 Liberty Drive
Bloomington, IN 47403
www.westbowpress.com
1 (866) 928-1240

ISBN: 978-1-5127-2602-2 (sc)
ISBN: 978-1-5127-2604-6 (hc)
ISBN: 978-1-5127-2603-9 (e)

Library of Congress Control Number: 2016900064

Print information available on the last page.

WestBow Press rev. date: 01/04/2016

About Camino Jim: I retired in 2008 after more than 30 years as a Manager in Financial Services. I then started my sales consulting business.

Tuesday, March 5, 2013
Turning 65...

I turned 65 yesterday. That's a good thing but it comes with conditions. First I get the feeling that others believe that 65 is a number which should mean that you must begin acting like you are not only older but that you should slow down and rest. Okay, I get it but I am not ready to just sit in the corner and be reminded that my napkin is on the floor or that I am now on Medicare.

So this will be the start of my notes for my 500 mile walk from St. Jean France to Santiago Spain, commonly referred to as The Camino Frances.

It is March 5th and if all goes well I will leave for Madrid on May 13th. That's 68 days from now. The original plan was to go in mid-August with Pat McFadden and John Pace. I feel terrible because it was Pat who got me thinking about The Camino. Pat had already made the decision to complete the "walk" and was kind enough to not only encourage me to join him but also was there to guide me through the process of getting my backpack and to start the training. If not for Pat I would not have become involved. Let me just point out that if something bad happens on the walk it was my choice. I have always tried to take responsibility for my decisions and that's not about to change.

I regret not being able to make the journey with Pat but I have concluded that I have as great a risk of injury or worse if I continue on my current training schedule for an additional three months. I could try to slow down now and then ramp up again in three months but I am convinced that if I slow down now I may lose what I have gained in the last three months and not get it back for an August departure. I have also become concerned that if I go backwards in my preparation I may get there in August and become an anchor to both Pat and John. While going alone is a real concern it does eliminate any risk of getting in the way of anyone else's pace. I have read a number of books and blogs about the Camino and all strongly suggest that you go at your own pace regardless of the pace or others. That is easier said than done. No one wants to be dragging behind or waiting for others to catch up. So as much as going alone is a bit scary I think it may be best for me and for Pat and John.

How long will it take? I don't know. I think it will take as long as it needs to. It is not a race, it's a journey. With the grace of God I will make it to the Cathedral of St. James in whatever time He allows. I don't care how long it takes; I just want to finish the entire 500 miles.

I have noticed an interesting variety or reactions from people when they hear about the Walk. It's not uncommon to hear "are you nuts" or a simple "why?" I have had a good number of people encourage me and express confidence in my ability to complete the task. That has been helpful, but I can't for the life of me understand how some people think I can do it when I myself am not all that sure.

I have also had a few people come right out and tell me that the idea is "crazy" or in one case I was told that "you will never make it". That comment has actually become a good motivator.

I am currently hiking about 40 miles each week with my backpack weighing in at about 23 pounds. The weight really depends on how much water I take along. Forty eight ounces of water is 4 pounds. I could take less because there is plenty of water available here but I need to carry the extra water in preparation for being in places where the water is in short supply or I just can't find it. Throw in three training sessions with Edwin at the gym each week and you can begin to see why I am concerned about running out of gas.

Most blogs suggest a daily average of 15 miles. That sounds fairly simple and straight forward but it does not take into account the weather and the terrain. For instance, the very first day from St Jean will require a walk of 15 miles but will also include an elevation change of 4,100 feet. The second day is also no bargain. The bottom line is that if you can survive the first two days without any major injuries or other problems you will significantly improve your chances of completing the Walk.

Walking 15 miles on flat terrain is hard; doing it up a hill of 4,100 feet is not the same. Throw in a little jet lag, a great deal of doubt and a fear of failure and the Walk starts to look like more than just averaging 15 miles a day and then flying home. While it may be just 15 miles in a day it's also 35 days in a row or with two days off its 37 days. Throw in the language issue and the real possibility of getting lost, sleeping in a group hostel in a bunk bed and finding food every day and you start to understand why people would ask "why?" It will be a great adjustment from years of being spoiled at some the world's best hotels. I doubt there will be a frequent visitor point system at a place in the middle of nowhere which charges 6 Euros for the night.

It's March 6th and tomorrow I need to put in at least 10 miles. It may rain so tomorrow may also be my first real test to see if I can properly pack with my rain cover, keep everything dry and still get in the 10 miles.

In my next update I will share my experience of hiking at the beach and being looked at like some kind of homeless guy. I think if I create a "will work for food" sign and pin it to my backpack I could make a few bucks. That's it for now.

Monday, May 6, 2013
Eye contact

I have been walking for hundreds of miles in my preparation for the Camino de Santiago and I have come to the conclusion that if you walk with a backpack, people often think you must be homeless or just a little off. After all, this is Southern California where no one walks anywhere on purpose.

I have had the distinct feeling that when walking with a backpack most people are trying to figure out what's wrong with you, where you are going and why your mode of transportation is on foot.

Because they think you are so weird, they also don't want to make eye contact with you. Maybe people are just not as friendly as they use to be. I'm not sure but I have noticed a difference in several types of people and their approach to or the avoidance of making eye contact with me while I am walking on the trail which ends at the beach.

It's become a game for me as I try to guess if the person or people walking toward me will say something like good morning, a simple nod, a smile, and a comment about the weather or really go out of their way to pretend you are invisible.

The vast majority will do everything they can to be looking away from me when we pass each other. When I sense that this will be their choice I will purposely move closer to the center of the path to see how they react. It's harder to pretend you don't see me if I am getting closer. I will often say "good morning" or "hi" just after we pass to see if they will respond. In most cases they don't. There are exceptions.

Most little kids just stare and smile while they are trying to figure out what that big thing is on my back or where I got that big stick I'm walking with. Teenagers would not stop to help even if I was on fire. As a group they are the most disgusting and their lack of manners is off the charts. I doubt this would have been the case ten years ago but the general decline of decency seems to be increasing at a much greater pace in this group.

The young between 20 somethings and the mid-thirties are about a 50/50 chance of a comment or eye contact. The young women have a much larger percentage that will say hello, good morning or have a nice day especially if they are alone.

The groups with the highest percentage who will make a comment are the people over 50. Maybe it's just the way they were raised.

There is one very unique individual who I have seen on the trail a couple of times. When I get to within about ten feet of him he always says "nice day isn't it". My answer is always the same, "yes it is". It's a unique encounter because he walks the path and he is blind. He has his red tipped stick and tends to hug the trail as closely to the right as possible perhaps because he wants to be sure there is plenty of room to get around him.

It's amazing that the one person I see often who would love to be able to make eye contact can't. From all that I have read about The Camino the interaction with others will be very different. I will soon find out.

Monday, May 6, 2013
The Countdown

Written last week...I leave in six days. I just returned from a one week visit to Arizona to play golf and visit with good friends. It was great to see the friends but my golf was less than stellar. Actually it was very poor, disappointing to say the least.

While I was there I did slack off in my training, getting in only one short walk of about six miles. I did however manage to get in lots of wine tasting practice. This part of training is now ahead of schedule.

I did "get back on the horse" today starting with a session with Edwin at the gym. After that session I hiked 7.5 miles with about 21 ponds and included a very good hill test at the 6 mile point. Surprisingly I did not have any issues or fatigue which I expected because of last week's training being what it was. That was encouraging but I also now have a lump behind my left knee which is a bit of a concern. I did ice it tonight and it seemed to help. I made an appointment to see my Doctor early tomorrow to see what he thinks. It seems like a simple fluid buildup which should be easy to fix. The real question is how to treat it while I am away if it flairs up again. This is just another part of "the journey".

Tomorrow I have another one hour session with Edwin and then 10 miles afterwards assuming the Doctor does not tell me to rest it or perhaps decides to treat it in a way which keeps me off the hike.

Getting close, it's hard to believe that I'm less than a week away from my departure.

Sunday, May 12, 2013
On my way tomorrow!

I'm on my way to The Camino. I fly tomorrow and I am glad the day has come. I will soon find out just how ready I am. I went to the Orthopedic Surgeon on Wednesday to look at the lump behind my left knee. The good news is that it's not a bone chip which would have been a real problem. It's a Baker's Cyst caused by straining a ligament which then gathers fluid and creates the lump. It will not go away and I know that it will reappear at the end of day one and stay with me for the entire journey. As long as it does not burst I will just have to deal with it. Ice will help but unfortunately I will be out in the country where ice is as hard to find as a Republican in California!

I have been writing about the training and my preparation and it's now time to go. I will keep in touch.

Wednesday, May 15, 2013
Arrival Day

I landed in Madrid in mid-afternoon after a flight of about 12 hours. I did get a little sleep but it's not easy for me when the cabin temperature is close to the same as Palm Desert.

I made my connection to Pamplona on a Turbo Prop which had 80 seats. My seat number was 2C. It was raining when we took our bus to the plane. When we arrived at the plane we boarded from the rear door so I walked to the front of the plane and sat in row 2 on the aisle. That was a mistake. It turns out that on this crop duster the rows are numbered from back to front so my seat was actually in the very back of the plane. I had already found an overhead spot for my backpack so I just left it because all of the space near my seat was now taken. It would only mean that I would just have to wait and let everyone get off the plane and them go and retrieve my backpack. A simple lesson in making assumptions on how things work; I need to remember that I am in Spain.

There are advantages to traveling with just a backpack. In spite of being the last person to get off the Turbo Prop I was the first person through the custom's checkpoint because I was not waiting for luggage. That was a first. The last time Robin and I went to Europe we took enough luggage to require two push carts to carry everything.

I made it to the hotel in Pamplona. It's time to get over the jet lag because tomorrow is the day to walk and find the Camino. I will be back in Pamplona at the end of my third walking day so I think I will just try to find where the Camino passes through so that I will have some idea on how to find this same hotel on Sunday. Enough for now.

Wednesday, May 15, 2013
Pamplona...Get past the jet lag and then make my way to St. Jean, France to start my 500 mile Camino journey.

I slept for a solid 8 hours which for me is rare. When I arrived yesterday in Pamplona it was sunny and hot. Yes hot. It was in the low 80's. When I woke this morning it was raining and cold. The temperature was in the 40's, what a change. I went online to look at the forecast for St. Jean, France where I will begin walking on Friday over the Pyrenees, an elevation increase of 4100 feet and by far the most difficult day. The forecast is for cold, wet weather, not good.

I quickly realized as I stepped out of the Hotel that I am not prepared for weather this cold and when you add in the elevation of the mountain it will be colder and if it is raining that just means that it will be much more difficult.

I decided to take a walk to find exactly where The Camino goes through Pamplona and was pleasantly surprised just how close my hotel is to where The Camino enters the city. It's only about 300 yards from the Hotel's front door. I was also surprised at how easy it was to find The Way as it is called. The streets have concrete scallop shells every 12 feet marking the path. Even I can't get lost on this part of The Camino. When you enter the city The Camino takes you right past the Cathedral of Pamplona dedicated to The Virgin Mary. I went in and said my first prayer on The Camino.

There were lots of Pilgrims walking through the city and I did see two pilgrim Albergue's one which had a sign that there were only two beds left for today. Yes, I am spoiled.

I stopped in at a Camino shop (I took a picture, actually several pictures but I have not yet figured out how to attach them) which is owned by a young couple from Budapest and they were very helpful in getting me fitted for my walking poles, a wool hat (a 2 Euro throwaway) to get me over the mountain, a Swiss Army knife and a pair of 6 Euro Blue sunglasses which they said I must have because it matches my rain jacket!

Back to the Hotel to drop off my new gear and then lunch at Hemingway's favorite bar. It's hard to not notice how things are different here. My lunch included a salad, steak with fries, dessert and wine with tip included all for 13.5 Euro. I good glass of wine at home would cost at least the same. I forgot to add that when the waiter brought the wine he just set down the bottle and that was it. Drink what you want, same price. I skipped the dessert and the waiter was shocked because it was all included. If I eat this way tomorrow I will be more concerned about the weight I will be dragging up the mountain and I'm not talking about the backpack! Time for a nap.

Thursday, May 16, 2013
Last day to prepare

I am preparing to leave for St Jean France on the other side of the Pyrenees to begin walking in the morning. The weather forecast is getting much worse and may become a problem including a delay. Once I arrive in St. Jean I will immediately head to the Camino office for information on the weather and if the route over the mountain is passable.

I met three pilgrims from San Diego last night at Hemingway's bar. They were all about my age, a married couple and the brother of the husband. The wife was born and raised in San Juan Capistrano about one mile from where we live—small world. They just completed the first three days and are taking the same route. They said that on the first day when they went over the mountain the weather was beautiful but after that it rained all day and it made it much more difficult.

Just an FYI about how the Banks operate here. I wanted to exchange US Dollars for Euro's and it was a real chore. When I asked the people at the front desk in my Hotel one of them immediately said that he would take me to the bank. The bank was just across the square and I could see the office easily. I told him that I could find it but he insisted on taking me. Once we got to the bank (Banco Popular) he surprised me when he came in with me. I soon found out why. Once in the bank he spoke to two different people at great length. The conversation was a bit animated and I thought that was unusual given the fact that all I wanted to do was exchange some Dollars for Euros. The next thing I know we are headed upstairs were my hotel front desk guy begins another conversation with a young woman who is clearly some kind of manager. That conversation ends and all three of us are headed back downstairs where another conversation of some length begins with a new person. Finally my hotel guy tells me that it's okay, but for not more than $200 US. He leaves.

I stand there for about another 15 minutes while the two managers push the keys on a computer keyboard and ask me for my US Passport. I comply. They make a photo copy and then ask me to sign three different documents none of which I have a clue about what they say or what I am signing. It dawns on me that after the manager takes my signed documents that for all I know I may now be in the Spanish Army! In the end the manager hands me 146 Euros and I leave the bank quickly before they change their mind. I can only imagine that if I had pushed for $500 US they would have had to call the Mayor's office.

That's it for now. I'm on my way to St. Jean to see what the plan will be.

Thursday, May 16, 2013
St Jean, France, the starting point for The Camino Frances to Santiago, Spain

I arrived in St. Jean from Pamplona this afternoon. My first stop was to have my Camino credential stamped and to get the latest on the weather at the top of the mountain. The weather when I arrived here was nice even with a little rain. The Camino center people told me that the path at the top had been closed today because of snow. The forecast for tomorrow is a bit like it was today. I will just have to get up early, pack and head to the Camino center to find out what the latest update is on the conditions. It will be a very long day.

I also found out today that as completely incompetent as my Spanish is it's much better than my French which simply does not exist. It's embarrassing to say the least. I started listening to a CD learning system called Spanish in Ten Minutes a Day. It helped, but for me I don't think 24 hours a day of listening to the CDs would have made me much better. Learning a language is for kids, us older guys just don't get it.

I had an early dinner at a small pizza place in the center of town and I met two guys who were traveling The Camino in reverse on bikes. They started in Portugal and now have more than 700 miles completed and are on their way to Switzerland. They are raising money for charity and when their trip is completed they will have covered more than 1000 miles. They are both from Vancouver and have passed through San Juan Capistrano on their bikes on the way to San Diego. I guess everyone I will meet has some connection to Capistrano.

This little town is crawling with people starting The Camino. I will just pick out a couple who look like they know where they are going and just follow them so that if I get lost I will have someone to blame.

It has been said that The Camino from St. Jean to Santiago is a journey of 1 million steps. I take my first step tomorrow at 7:30.

Friday, May 17, 2013
The first day St. Jean France to Roncesvalles, Spain

Wow, what a start. I have been thinking about this day since the first time a read about it. Every blog, book or guide you can find will tell you that this first stage is the most difficult and therefore it is the one stage I have had serious doubts about. At one time I considered starting in Pamplona to avoid this stage. It would just mean walking 450 miles not 500. That would still be a real challenge, right?

Every time I thought about it I came away with one concern. If I skipped the most difficult stage would I have doubts about the journey and always wonder if I could I have done it? There was no choice; I had to start in St. Jean.

Fast forward to my arrival day and the weather forecast is dreadful and the mountain route has been altered and at the Camino office I am told that last week a man from Brazil died on the mountain when he fell to his death while trying to go over the mountain in bad conditions. So here I am today at 5:15 in the morning, I open the window and it is raining cats and dogs with a temperature of about 47 degrees. I go on the internet and the forecast is for the rain to fall all day with some fog and a high temperature of 57. Wow, what to do.

I begin packing for the rain and get all of my rain gear out including a wool cap, gloves and my thermal survival blanket ready to go. Well at 5:40 my cell phone gives off that sound that a message has arrived. I check and it's from a very close friend of Robin's, Debbie, and it says "I am praying for no rain tomorrow. You go Jim". I respond "it's raining cats and dogs pray harder". Of course I am joking.

I am now packed and dressed for the worst. I leave the Hotel, it is 6:30 and as I step out of the building the rain stops. I walk across the street to a little cafe for coffee and a pastry and I just wait for the rain to return but it does not. I leave and walk to the Camino starting point and as I take my first step the sun comes out! Amazing, just amazing. I walk The Camino for seven hours in sunshine. I stop after the first hour to take off all of my extra weather gear and clothing because I am sweating like it is summer.

The weather is perfect for my entire walk and as I approach my destination, the village of Roncesvalles it starts to rain lightly, just as a reminder of just how blessed I am.

Thank you Debbie and thanks to so many others who wished me well and sent messages praying that I would have great weather and a great journey. I made it! Thank you Debbie and to all of the many who have wished me well.

It's time to get a glass of wine and something to eat. More later.

Friday, May 17, 2013
First day gatherings

Once I started walking The Camino without the fear of spending the entire day laboring in the rain I found myself able to concentrate on why I am here. The first thing I noticed was that walking for hours in an environment completely foreign to me allowed me to just take it all in. When I was training for this trip in Capistrano I would walk the same route, see or be avoided by the same people and the environment was always the same. I did not try to see things differently. I was just on a mission to walk a required number of miles carrying a designated number of pounds in my backpack for training purposes. Today was very different.

I noticed everything. I had no choice because it was all new and new meant interesting. Not only was the environment different, all of the people were new and different. The people were also different in another way. They were interested in you if for no other reason than to meet new people or to simply ask..."Why are you on The Camino?" In most of my conversations people don't ask but instead they just want to tell you why they are here and then they will ask you. The focus is to unveil something. The woman sitting next to me tonight at the Pilgrims dinner told me (unsolicited) that she had just lost her job two weeks ago and only then decided that she would join her Husband on his planned Camino. Interesting that she thought that if she began to look for new work she might find something and that would mean not being able ask a new employer for 5 weeks of vacation at the start of the new job. Did her husband want to go alone? Was it his idea or was he asked? None of my business, but it left me wanting to ask those questions and of course I could not.

The two French women and their male companion sitting directly across from me were completely uninterested in anything to do with anyone. I got the impression that they were either just not going to deal with language issues or they decided that a dinner which included wine for ten Euro was worth having to avoid eye contact with me. It worked until the meal arrived.

The dish contained two items, French fries and a whole trout. Yes a whole trout, head to tail, bones included. I cut open the side of the fish and took a small bite which turned out to be mostly tiny bones. I knew then that I had finished eating the trout because after walking from St. Jean successfully I was not going to die choking on a fish bone. The French women sitting across from me was very amused with my lack of effort because it now gave her the ability to remove the bone from her trout completely while at the same time maintaining eye contact with me and never looking down on her work. I assume she was not trying to show me how but rather it was her goal to just remind me that she could and I could not. How do these people find me?

In the end she and her companions got what they wanted, a dinner with wine for ten Euro and the chance to sit across from an ignorant American. Well done.

Two things are for sure. One, I will most likely attend another Pilgrim meal and two I will make sure that I am not sitting in the company of any of these people ever again. I ate little and learned much, they eat more and learned nothing.

If all of the Pilgrim meals include a whole fish I will be losing more weight than I can imagine. Good night.

Saturday, May 18, 2013
The rain (but not snow) in Spain Falls Mainly on the Plain

It will be difficult to truly describe today but I will do my best. It was 6:00 am when I woke and looked out the one window of my tiny room. I was shocked. Everything was white and it was snowing sideways. Do I go? Am I prepared for this?

Answer, no choice, I go. First I have a little breakfast which is basically bread, ham and coffee. The coffee is so strong that it will keep you awake regardless of how tired you think you are. That will actually help today. I pack and arrange all of my gear and I am now dressed for the weather as best I can be. Frankly I never had a snow storm in my planning.

As I first get started it really looks beautiful but that's only because I have not yet set foot on the trail. Stage 3 today will be 21.2 km or about 13 miles nearly all down some very steep terrain. Here is what my guide book says "be careful of the steep descent into Zubiri - the exposed rock makes it very slippery, particularly in wet conditions". I guess that includes a snow storm.

So I start and the first thing I notice is that nearly all of the branches of the trees overhanging the path are now at waist level because of the heavy wet snow. I will be going under, around and just plain through these limbs for the next five hours. I did not know it then and I must admit that if someone told me that it would continue to snow hard for the next 5 hours I'm not sure I would have gone. But I did. In the end I will be on the trail today with it snowing for the first 5 hours and steady rain for the last three hours at the lower elevation.

This day will turn out to be the most difficult day I have ever had. Yesterday was supposed to be the toughest day and I can now say that today was far more difficult because of the weather. If I did not have my walking poles I would have spent most of the day on my butt or worse. I came to a small pond and the only way around it was to climb a small group of very large rocks at the edge of the pond. I took it very slowly and as I reached the last step I lost my footing and if not for the poles I would have been in the pond. I could not avoid throwing myself in the other direction and ended up with both my feet in about 6 inches of water. My feet were now completely soaked. I have 9 miles to go. It was going to get worse because I had not yet reached the steep decline ahead of me.

Mud weighs more than water. I can testify to that. The trail was a mess and as you slog through the mud your shoes just get heavier with each step. As a result I find myself trying to find small puddles of water to rinse off the mud and reduce the weight. Why not, my feet are as wet as they can be so it seems like an easy choice. Not a problem. The trail ultimately becomes a little river as the water from the higher elevation finds its way down the trail.

Hard to believe, but along the way when you step out into a clearing it's really beautiful. I stopped to take pictures which I have sent to Robin. I also took a few of what the trail looked like.

Five hours into the march it starts to get very steep and very slippery. Every step is a potential for something very bad. I slow down and just keep telling myself that caution here is most important, not time.

There are really no other small villages on the way to Zubiri so I just keep pushing along. I pass a number of others on the trail, some of whom are clearly struggling. I do come across a very interesting couple who have stopped to take a picture of each other with a valley covered in snow as a backdrop. I ask if they would like me to take a picture of them together not have any clue as to what language they might speak. As luck would have it the big guy speaks up and in an instant I know where he's from—either Ireland or Scotland. I take a guess and I ask him if he's from Ireland. He looks at me and pulls up his rain cover which goes nearly from head to toe and he's wearing a kilt! I would have asked him to let me take his picture but any man tough enough to wear a kilt in these conditions is not a man you want to run the risk of making angry.

This is some journey!

As I get closer to Zubiri my mind is completely focused on two things. The first is to be sure that at this late stage in today's walk I remind myself not to speed up and make a careless mistake which could be end of my Camino. The second is on the village of Zubiri with a population of only about 200 people. There will not be many options for places to stay. I asked Sharel to see if she could find something and when I did I gave her the wrong dates and only realized it a week ago. This could be impossible to say the least. I am now approaching Zubiri and I recall an email from her I received after I left and she said she had found something but I am not sure if it was booked.

As the true professional she took the lead and booked it while I was on my way to Madrid. I didn›t know that for sure so I am exhausted and can only think about what I will do if I am without a place to stay. I wrote down the name of the place before I started this morning and as I enter town there is a pilgrim›s Albergue where people are trying to get a bunk bed but it› sold out. I go in and finally a guy working there asks me if he can help. I hand him the slip of paper with the name of the place on it and he tells me to turn right and go about a quarter of a mile and it will be on the left. I am looking for the Gautxori Hotel. I still have no idea if there will be a room for me. There are no other rooms in Zubiri, including bunk beds. I find it. I walk into what looks like a bar. There are a bunch of old guys playing cards and the bartender looks at me and begins to ask me questions is Spanish. All I can do is show him what I wrote down on the paper. He puts one finger in the air which I think he is doing to ask me to wait. He grabs a book from under the bar and begins looking at a list of names. I point to my name on the paper; he shakes his head and then looks up and says "yes"!

The Gautxori has just become the Zubiri Four Seasons! He shows me to my room and I could care less what it looks like. Thank you Sharel.

I begin to unpack only to discover that my REI rain cover for my backpack did not deliver. Nearly everything in my backpack is wet. I really don't care. I start hanging everything all over the place. Unlike any other Four Seasons I have stayed in, my Zubiri Four Seasons has two radiators which will really help to start the drying process. I empty my boots of the water, put them back on and return to the bar. I am really hungry. I have not eaten anything on the trail.

The people who work at this converted Motel could not have been nicer. I immediately get the impression that they know what I have just been through. I had the best misto salad and a razor thin steak and I am in heaven. I go back to my room and fall asleep for four hours and when I wake up I feel great, no pains no issues with my feet. My shoulders are sore but it's clear that the training has paid off.

I don't know what tomorrow will be like but I think I can say it will be easier. Pamplona is next. Good night.

Sunday, May 19, 2013
On my way to Pamplona

I woke this morning at 7:45 (I slept in) and the first thing I did was check to see if all of my gear had dried out from yesterday's adventure. The good news is yes and the bad news is that all of the laundry I did in the bathroom sink also was dry. Robin gave me a bunch of Tide washing packets and told me how to use them and it worked perfectly. Why is that bad news? It's not; it's just a confession about my new laundry skills.

It's actually funny because I know that when this is read by a number of people there will be a collective gasp at this confession. I can only imagine how many people will be grinning from ear to ear with the thought of me doing laundry in a Hotel bathroom sink. I know that at least Maggie, Alyce, Charles, Gary and Debbie are getting a good laugh from this.

I say that because when we all worked together I was so spoiled that when I traveled I would take with me my own shower head and wrench because I insisted on water pressure. They all thought that was a riot.

Ok. Part of this journey is to live outside of my comfort zone and clearly I am making progress. The Zubiri Four Seasons was a start and now it's the laundry. With that out of the way you can all now just imagine that at the end of each day's walk I begin the recovery process with this new skill.

Alright that is enough about the laundry. After checking the condition of all my things I peek out the window to see what I will face today. Surly it can't be anything like yesterday. I am correct. It's chilly. I know that because unlike any other Four Seasons in the world the Zubiri Four Seasons has a sign out front which continuously updates the time and temperature as a public service. It's 7:46 and the sign says its 12. I know that's cold in "F" and I believe that in "C" that's still not warm. It's raining lightly and it's not sunny. No big deal. After yesterday I am ready for Zubiri to have its first tornado.

I pack and dress with multiple layers because 12 "C" just has to be cold. It is a little. I find this out as I make my way to breakfast (included) because unlike all other Four Seasons the Zubiri Four Seasons requires you to exit the building to access the dining room, aka the bar to get your pre-paid meal. I enter and place my backpack between the cigarette machine and the jukebox. How many of you have ever been able to say that? This journey will continue to provide a countless number of "firsts" this being one of them.

Breakfast of course includes some eye opening real coffee not the stuff we in the US think is coffee. No, this is not Starbucks, this is the real deal. In addition to the coffee I am given a basket of bread and a very sizable croissant. Apparently the Spanish like to carb up to start the day. I agree and eat most of it with real butter. I thank my host and grab my backpack and step out into the rain. At home I would be running from the rain but after yesterday it's really nice. As I head toward Church I pass a family of five on donkeys going who knows where. This in Southern California would make the "breaking news" segment at nine. I take a picture which I will send as soon as I figure out how to do it.

As I reach the church I am disappointed to find that all of the doors are locked. It's Sunday so this can't be right. I look and there is a sign which lists all of the Church's Mass's and there is only one each day. The Sunday Mass is at 11:00 am. All other Masses are at 6:00 pm daily. That makes sense. With a population of 500 (I said in yesterday's message that there were only 200, my guidebook says 500) there is no way to keep the Church open and have it maintained with all of the cost to do so. That's okay I will just find another on the way. Wrong. There are no others along the way. I am out in the middle of a forest where people still ride donkeys in the center of town. Then I will just wait until I arrive in Pamplona.

The travel is fairly easy. I don't want to get ahead of myself but this is just not like the first two days. Yes it's raining a little but it's just not a problem. I am beginning to adjust the way I see things like rain. It's no big deal and it's natural. I get it, we really don't need umbrellas.

The real challenge today is mud and lots of it. From time to time along the Camino today I will find myself with conditions which cannot be ignored without penalty. Along the trail there are spots where the width of the trail is about two feet wide and it's like walking in chocolate pudding.

I make my way to Larrasoana a village with a population of 200. Yes 200 as stated in my guide book. Larrasoana wants to be Zubiri when it grows up. The trail takes you right through the village. I see a sign that says Market and it has an arrow pointing in a direction opposite of where the trail will start again. Why not, I will go and buy something to take with me for lunch, a snack and perhaps a bottle of flavored water or a Gatorade. As I walk the 500 meters (the sign said it was 500 meters) it dawns on me that if all of the churches are closed on Sunday why am I now thinking that the one and only market In this sprawling metropolis is going to be open.

I find it. There is a hand written note complete with arrow pointing to a button and it says "push". I can't believe that I am dumb enough to do it but I do. I push the button and instantly the lights inside go on and this guy rushes to open the door and greets me with "Buenos Dias".

I grab a freshly baked loaf of French bread, thinly sliced ham, a banana and two bottles of the Spanish version of Gatorade. It cost next to nothing. I pay him and before I leave he tells me (his English is near perfect) that I should avoid the next 3k on the trail because of the damage from the storm and just walk on the side of the road. He goes on to tell me that it is Sunday and therefore there will be little traffic. I take his advice.

All is going fine for about 10 minutes when the first car is coming toward me. It goes by me like an Indy car! I don't know how fast it's going but I don't think it was within any speed limit I have ever driven. For those of you who are not up on your miles vs."K's" let me just point out that I will now be walking head on into Indy Car racing for the next 1.8 miles. This is what happens when you try to cut corners on the advice of a guy who owns a market in a village with a population of 200 people. Bring back the mud!

The balance of the day is uneventful. I was surprised that the last 3-4 miles was spent walking through neighborhoods in the outskirts of the city. It was a good day. No stress, no physical issues. I posted a picture of my walking boots which I now call my Limos. I think it's on the blog. I'm not very good at this. I think the picture is interesting because it will help you visualize what the front desk guy's face at my Hotel in Pamplona looked like when Mr. Mud walked across his freshly polished lobby floor. By the way even the Cathedral was closed when I walked past it as I entered the center of the city.

Tomorrow on to stage 4, a short walk of about ten miles but with a very steep climb up through the middle of a large collection of wind turbines to the town of Puente La Reina.

That's it for now and don't forget…don't stray from the chosen path.

Monday, May 20, 2013
Stage 4 on to Puente La Reina with the Cheaters!

Get a glass of wine this could take a while.

I started today thinking that I was looking at a walk of about 10.5 miles but I was wrong. I was looking at the distance from Cizur Menor which is closer than Pamplona which meant that today would actually be about 14 miles.

Before I get started on today I first need to share with something I left out of yesterday's summary. I left it out because I was ashamed of what took place. I have since reconciled and in the end I trust you will agree with me. This time walking alone gets you to really think about a lot of the things you did or did not do at some point in your life.

If you read my walk to Pamplona blog you may recall that I stopped in a very small market, had to ring a bell to get in and after helping me the owner talks me into taking a short cut for 3km on what turns out to be the Indianapolis Speedway. Here is what I did not share with you.

When I gathered the few things I bought at his market I paid him and he handed me my change which was a bunch of coins. I have no idea what their value was. I then offered them back to him as a thank you, a tip, a gratuity but he refused and instead he said to me "give it to someone you meet on The Camino who needs it".

I get to Pamplona and after I finish taking care of my gear and take a shower I need something to eat. I ask the front desk person for a recommendation and he tells me that because it is Sunday most restaurants are closed but the Hemingway place just 100 feet away is open. Perfect. I stroll over there and just as I am reaching for the door there appears this middle aged guy with a paper cup in his hand between me and the restaurant. I ignore him. He says something to me but I have no idea what he is saying to me as I enter the bar. I am not really sure…was he asking me for money? Was that just a cup of coffee in his hand? What did he say to me?

I am half way through a beer and suddenly I am in a panic. Remember... "Give it to someone you meet on The Camino who needs it". I missed it. I feel just terrible. I pay for the beer and go outside hoping to find him and make things right but I can't find him. It's a very busy plaza with lots of outdoor sidewalk cafes. Surly if he is asking people for money this is a place where he could find people who would have money to give him. I do two laps around the plaza but to no avail. He is gone. I feel terrible as I return to the restaurant for dinner.

When I get back to my room I convince myself that while my first decision was not good my efforts to find him and make good on my conversation with the guy at the market does make me feel better.

I have now committed that before I complete The Camino I will "give it to someone on The Camino who needs it". There will be a better end to this story.

Here's where today's title comes from. While at the Hemingway bar a guy sitting next to me asks if I am on The Camino. I tell him yes. He asks me where I am staying. I tell him at La Perla right next door. The next question is a strange one. Are you taking your luggage? Yes, I have a backpack. Long story short he explains that there are people who walk The Camino and have a courier service which takes their luggage from one location to the next. La Perla is a very nice Hotel and I guess he just assumed that if I am staying there and walking The Camino I might be one of the cheaters, my word not his. I wonder if their credentials are stamped with an *? Hey don't get me wrong, walking 500 miles is still no picnic but doing it with 23 pounds on your back is another story. I think their stamps should be different. This is just one opinion.

So now finally I'm on to today. It's 4:00 am and I am wide awake. I can't sleep. I am exhausted but it does not matter. I am not sure if it's a delayed reaction to jet lag or the effects of the coffee I had three days ago. I can't read anymore because my eyes are killing me and I need some eye drops to help. That story will come later.

Can't sleep might as well turn on the television. It takes me less than a minute to surf all 8 channels to choose from. Here are my choices: There are six game shows on with lots of color, flashing lights and loud music. There is also a professional ping-pong match or a diving contest. So there is nothing to watch, but at least the search is over in less than a minute. It's not like home where you have to search 340 channels to reach the same conclusion. Spanish television is easier.

I have all of my gear selected for the day and I am nearly finished with packing. I head to breakfast. First I stop in the lobby to ask what time the pharmacy will open and I am told 9:00. Okay, breakfast now. It's a carb fest as usual along with a couple of pieces of fruit.

I return to my room complete the packing and reduce one layer of clothing because it's already a beautiful day and the forecast for the entire day is good. It's just about nine and my good friend who last week escorted me to the bank is on duty. I explain that I need some eye drops. He says he will take me and explain to the clerk what is needed. The pharmacy is directly across from the hotel. It's not 50 feet from the front door. We go and he does all the talking. The woman at the pharmacy asks if I have an infection. I say "no" and she reaches into a cabinet and hands me Vispring, it's the international version of the product, Visine.

I am now good to go. I thank him for all of his help and I head to The Camino, Puente La Reine is about 14 miles away. It's a drop dead beautiful day and I have taken many pictures which I will put on

Facebook or some other place once I figure out how to do it. As I am about to leave Pamplona I pass a bank and decide to try the ATM. It works. No more ordeals at the bank trying to exchange dollars. So far this day is really going well. I have eye drops, cash and the weather is perfect. What could possibly go wrong?

It's not long before I see the first challenge. It's a hill. A very, very long hill and it just keeps going up. I can't see the end of it. I stop at the bottom and I say The Lord's Prayer and I go. So now you know what my secret weapon is. I have done this from day one each time I am faced with a difficult challenge and so far I have faced some tough ones and I have overcome each of them. From this point on you will know what I was doing whenever I mention a real challenge.

I take the hill without a stop and I pass a number of people. Little do I know what's ahead of me; there is a long and beautiful trail which is taking me to the real challenge. The Hill of Forgiveness, Alto del Perdon. It's very difficult and there is no taking this hill in one shot. I stop many, many times not just because the hill is so tough, but also because the scenery is spectacular. I can only hope that a few of the pictures can do it justice. What I don't know when I finally reach the top is what's on the other side. The climb has taken me up about 1200 feet but the decent will be much tougher.

It's windy at the top of the hill and I take a short break sitting beneath one of the wind turbines. They are huge and they are ugly. It's windy so I stop only briefly. That was a mistake. I should have rested to face the decent.

The trail for most of the next hour and a half is nothing but rocks of all shapes and sizes. Not little friendly stones, rocks. This is where the use of your poles is the only way to get down. I find out later when I reach Puente La Reina that when you are walking downhill like this it shifts the weight of your backpack from your hips to your shoulders.

At the end of the decent it's another 10km to my destination. When I arrive I will finally begin to feel the effects on my shoulders, especially my left shoulder.

I reach my hotel, El Cerco. I cannot wait to dump my backpack. I get to my room and crash. It's about 4:00 in the afternoon so this stage took about six and a half hours. It was sneaky tough. I take care of all of my gear, shower and then go to get something to eat. I am so sore that I can hardly lift my left arm. I order something which does not require the use of a knife, a sandwich. It does not take long to finish because I just want to get back to the room to sleep and rest this shoulder.

I am asleep at 5:30 and I wake up at 10:30. I feel better and the Advil is kicking in. Tomorrow I walk to Estella a journey of nearly 15 miles. There is one steep climb early in the day, but it's nothing like today and certainly nothing like today's decent.

How was your wine? I warned you. I think I'll watch some ping-pong. Good night.

Tuesday, May 21, 2013
No sun glasses today...It's going to rain

I am packed and ready to go at 7:30 but first I will head downstairs for my carb boost. Before I leave the room I take a look out my window to check the weather. It's gray, very gray and it looks cold. Once I am carbed up I will step outside to see what it's like and then make any final wardrobe adjustments.

It's going to rain. I know it. I am now a professional forecaster. Maybe when I get back to Southern California I can get one of those really cushy jobs telling people that for the foreseeable future it's going to be sunny with temperatures ranging from 71 to 72. They get paid for this. They should come here and see what it's like to see the weather change from day to day, minute to minute. Ok, I will need to make a couple of changes which will include putting my backpack rain cover on before I leave.

Since we are on the subject of rain covers you may recall that on that dreadful snow and rain day I mentioned that all of the gear in my backpack was wet because of an REI equipment failure. Well that was incorrect and I apologize to REI. I realized my error this morning when I put on the cover exactly as I did on day 2 and just before I put the backpack on I noticed that there was a substantial gap on the side of the cover. Simply, I had put it on incorrectly. The REI equipment was not the problem it was an operator error. My excuse? I have been training for this journey in Southern California and I never walked in the rain! How could I? It never rains. My lack of practice was the cause of the problem not the equipment. I should also point out that while I am on a boost REI attempt at making amends for my false criticism of their product I just want to go on record that my Limos were purchased at REI and they have been the best investment I have made for The Camino. There, that should set the record straight.

Before I tell you what the first thing that happens to me when I step out of the Hotel Cerco let me first go to 1:30 am.

I slept from about 5:30 to 10:30. I just crashed. My shoulder was hurting and I was really tired. I wake up at 10:30 and I feel much better and the Advil is working. I can't get back to sleep so I decide I will go to my guide book and take a more detailed look at what's coming in stage 5 to Estella.

I look at my Hotel booking. I am staying at the Tixmista Hotel in Estella (Navarra) but everything I am looking at in my guide book refers to Estella (Lizarra). The guide book by John Brierley is priceless and as important as my passport. In each destination the guide book lists all of the Albergue's available only to Camino Pilgrims. In addition the guide goes into great detail about "Other Accommodations". I read it over and over and I cannot find my Hotel, the Hotel Tixmista listed anywhere nor does it appear on the maps provided in the guide for Estella.

Oh no. Are there two Estella's? Estella Navarra and Estrella Lizarra? Have I given Sharel the wrong Estrella? I don't handle these kinds of situations very well. It's 1:30 in the morning so I send Robin an email asking if she can figure this out. Robin was a travel professional, meeting planner for 16 years so she knows how to navigate these problems and her tech skills are as good as it gets. She can figure it out. I don't want to contact Sharel because I have already driven her crazy by giving her a list of Hotels but with the wrong dates of arrival so this needs to be fixed without her getting any additional evidence that I am a terrible customer.

Within a minute Robin is back to me and has found my Hotel on Google Earth and forwarded the map and all of the details on how to get there once I exit The Camino. I am saved. Thank God for Robin and a 9 hour time change!

This brings me to another subject previously discussed in my ramblings. Remember the "cheaters"? Well I have given this some additional thought and I was wrong in my comments about their credential being stamped with an *. Why the change of opinion? Because I am also a cheater if we really want to get down to the real Camino Pilgrims.

I stay in Hotels and have resources at my disposal to fix my problems almost instantly but the real "Pilgrims" are those who stay in the Albergue's. They sleep in rooms with as many as 100 strangers in bunk beds, share bathrooms and showers and the list goes on of all the things I am not doing. So from this point on I will discontinue referring to anyone on The Camino as "cheaters" for traveling The Camino in whatever way they choose. There are no cheaters.

So now that I have cleared up those issues let's get to today and my 15 miles to Estella. I leave the Hotel Cerco after my daily carb fix and step out into the street on my way to The Camino. I am greeted by a group of about six or seven kids on their way to school and they all appear to be about the same age as my grandson Brayden who is 7. Without exception they all greet me with smiling faces all with their little school backpacks with "Buenos Dias". It's a very cold morning and the sky is threatening but I am off to a great start.

The Camino is a short distance away and as you head out of the city you walk over the bridge which was renamed Queens Bride in honor of its benefactor Dona Mayor wife of Sancho the third. Today will be a different challenge.

At the start the trail climbs but not anything like the elevation changes I have encountered in the first 4 stages. This will be a cold, windy and gray different test. All of the stress related to the elevation comes early. I welcome the less difficult climb.

When I first arrived in Estella I was tired and my shoulders were very sore especially my left shoulder. I feel pretty good and again I come to realize that regardless of how you feel at breakfast once you get an hour in and heat up all of your muscles your discomfort is gone. Today is no different.

Today's walk is quite and regardless of the conditions its good thinking weather. I think I already warned you about this time to think issue especially with me doing the thinking. Who else could find a connection between The Camino and NASCAR? Leave it to me.

I have been to one NASCAR event in my life as the guest of a very good friend in Phoenix AZ. It was great fun and we did it like "cheaters". We had a big fancy bus with all of the trappings. So how can I connect The Camino to this?

It occurred to me today that I am seeing the same people every day and on a day like today even more frequently. Here's the NASCAR connection. When you watch a NASCAR event the cars race around the track in less than 25 seconds per lap, you soon realize that there are cars on every part of the track. Who's in first, third or last? It's hard to keep track even with the giant pole in the center of the track that shows the car numbers for the top ten or so. Regardless, how can you find them when they are traveling at 200 miles an hour?

Pit stops! That's the key. When the leader goes into the pit for tires and fuel he will be passed by the second place car unless they go to the pits at the same time. Make sense? It's the same on The Camino. I pass a bunch of people who have stopped to take off their shoes (aka tires) and drink something (aka fuel). There will soon be a point where I will stop for a drink (fuel) and perhaps an equipment adjustment (aka tires) and when I do I will see the same people I passed an hour ago pass me.

It's not a race, at least not for me and I believe not for the vast majority on The Camino. The only real difference is that none of the people I see and or pass on The Camino have all of the NASCAR sponsor logos or a number on their backpack. Perhaps there's an opportunity to get Go Daddy or Budweiser involved in The Camino!

I can see it now. In addition to your credential you would be assigned a number and if lucky a couple of sponsors who think you can finish. Nike could give you the shoes, REI the gear and Columbia your clothing. I think I'm on to something here.

Ok. Where was I? The balance of the walk was just quiet and pleasant in spite of the cold. I walked through vineyards, olive groves and beautiful little villages on my way to Estella. I was about five miles from Estella when it started to rain a bit more heavily. It was perfect timing for me because there was a tiny Albergue and a cafe-bar at the top of the hill. I stopped in. Trying my best to order something in Spanish I pointed (it's okay to point) at a sandwich which I wanted and tried to order it in Spanish, my best Spanish and she handed me a different one. I just took it. My Spanish is just not very good.

La Bodega Del Camino was doing a very nice business. If I had waited for just a minute or two longer I would have seen the pasta being delivered to the table of three next to me and I would not now be stuck with this sandwich. I did, however, successfully order my Cerveca. This tiny place also has an Albergue and free Wi-Fi. I finish my speed lunch and start the final five miles to Estella. The day has been overcast and with rain showers off and on but now it's starting to pick up. There is also a noticeable drop in the temperature and the wind is more challenging. I am just hoping I can reach my Hotel before this turns into a more serious storm.

I have a map and it shows me that the Hotel Tixmista is a long way from where I will be leaving The Camino. I am trying my best to figure out which plaza is which but the streets are so narrow and with the massive stone structures it is impossible to see anything that might be found on my map. It's raining so I duck under the cover of a building where I am now trying to find a street name, any name on the map. No luck. At that moment a well-dressed older man asks me in perfect English "do you speak English, can I help you"?

I hand him my map and the piece of paper with the name of the Hotel Tixmista on it to him and he appears to be confused. He then politely stops a young woman to look at the map and they share information. The woman then points directly over my shoulder and makes several hand gestures, smiles and leaves. He thanks her, I thank her.

My new found guide in perfect English tells me to walk to the end of the road I am standing on pointing behind me, look for the Hospital and then turn left and the Hotel will be a short distance from there. I thank him several times and about 15 minutes later I am standing in the Hotel lobby. Let me just say that the Spanish people I have met have all gone out if their way to help me. They are a very nice people.

Today›s walk has taken about seven hours and I am ready to eat something which requires both a fork and knife.

I check in, take care of my gear and head down stairs to see what the restaurant serves. I ask for a menu and before the front desk clerk (he does multiple tasks) brings it to me he points out that the restaurant does not open until 8:30. It's now 4:30. I ask if there are any other places nearby and he tells me that the Yerri hotel has food now and it's just a short walk.

I get to the Yerri hotel and bar and all they have are the same sandwiches I had yesterday and at lunch today. I need something better, you know like something cooked. I decide to go for a walk. Yes, I just walked about 14 miles and now I'm going for a stroll. It's getting colder and I make sure I don't stray from the path I am on to be sure I don't need help getting back. I can't find anything which serves before 8:30. I head back to the Hotel.

With two hours to go I will just take a glass of wine to my room and read while I wait. I fall asleep never touching the wine and luckily I wake at about 8:45. Perfect. I make my way back to the restaurant and the waiter-desk clerk who poured me the glass of wine two hours ago has noticed that I have returned with the same glass of wine. He looks confused.

Dinner is a small plate of pasta to start and a sirloin with spinach. It's cooked, hot and good. I am ready to get some sleep.

Tomorrow I am off to Los Arcos which will have some early challenges and a total distance of 13.1 miles. Good night.

Wednesday, May 22, 2013
I just arrived in Los Arcos and I am in the back seat of a Police car!

Ok, more on the Police later. Let's start with the beginning of the day. I slept well last night and did not wake until 7:00.

As always the first thing I do is open the window and get a feel for the weather. It's chilly, but it's not raining. Not yet. The sky is dark and it sure looks like it is going to rain so I pack accordingly.

I'm getting pretty good at this packing stuff. It's actually easy once you get the hang of it. For instance anything you are certain you will not need between destinations simple goes in first at the bottom of the backpack and anything you are sure you want access to is available at the top of the backpack or in the lid which will let you get to whatever it is quickly.

Today it looks like it will rain so I have my rain pants readily available. My guide book, passport, credential, cash, credit cards are all in Zip Lock bags and they are all in the top flap. Also in the top flap might be a snack or something to eat along the way. I also have my iPad mini in a Zip Lock with its charger connector and the Spanish adaptor at the top of the backpack. Those items are never separated from each other, never.

My medications which I take before I leave the Hotel are in Zip Locks and then put into a water proof shaving kit. Before I finish packing I go over a check list to be sure that at worst the critical, non-replaceable items are not left behind. As a side note I take every one of the critical items with me whenever I leave the room. They are never out of my control. I just fill my pockets, the ones with zippers and they are always with me without exception.

I can only imagine the smile on the faces of the guys I play golf with. Mike must be just shaking his head in disbelief. I have played a lot of golf with Mike and he has become the guardian of my "stuff". He will ask me five or six times when we play if I have my cell phone, my keys and anything else I have brought along. He knows me all too well.

So now that I have packed I am ready for the morning carb fest. I am shocked to see that today scrambled eggs are available. That's an easy decision. I also order my coffee con leche. That's coffee with milk. It's very good coffee and better than anything I have had at home. I wonder what would happen if I asked for decaf? I can only imagine the shock. You want coffee that's not coffee? Might even be a crime here.

I am having breakfast and my email kicks in letting me know I have a message. The Wi-Fi did not work in my room last night so I'm getting messages sent from yesterday or whatever day it is at home.

It's from Wally B a good friend and he tells me that he took my advice that came with my blog that started with "Get a glass of wine this could take a while". He goes on to say that he is reading my blog with a glass of Camus Special Select and that this follows a wine session with Tony and John. Trust me these guys don't need any encouragement.

I finish breakfast and get ready to take on this stage to Los Arcos a walk of 13.1 miles. I gather my things but I am missing something

(I can just imagine the look on Mike's face). It's my hat. I look all around my table but there is no hat. Not a problem I must have left it in the room. That's okay it's not one of the critical items. I return to my room for the hat. It's not there. I look everywhere but it's gone. No big deal I will just find a place that sells baseball hats as I make my way to The Camino.

I am now at the front desk checking out and asking the desk clerk for directions back to The Camino. I know it's at least a half mile or more. She is very nice and takes out a map and begins to trace my route with a pen. She stops and circles the location of a market. She makes special circles around its location clearly indicating that if I fail to recognize this market and do not turn left at that point it will not be good. I thank her and turn to leave. She calls out "Senior". I turn around and she is holding my hat. I don't ask and she does not say how. Regardless I have my hat. I head for The Camino, its 9:15.

I walk for about ten minutes and I start thinking that I should be near this market where I must turn left. Did I pass it? I'm thinking that a "market" here is very different from a Ralph's. This could be a place the size of a small dry cleaner at home. I'm sure I missed it but first I will check the map she gave me and try to identify a landmark or a street name, something. I am standing there looking at my map and in less than ten seconds a voice simply says "Camino".

I turn and its and old man just staring at me and he repeats "Camino", but this time I know he is asking me if I am trying to find it. I say "Si". He then reaches out takes a look at my map and turns and waves for me to follow him. We walk about three blocks; nothing else is said between us. He takes me across the street at a crosswalk and hands me back my map and points over my shoulder and for the third time since I have known him he says "Camino" and walks away. He heads back in the direction of where he found me. This total stranger just walked with me for three blocks to be sure I found my way. God these people are nice!

I find The Camino and I am on my way to Los Arcos. My guide book tells me that most of the elevation change will come early probably in the first four miles of this thirteen mile segment.

The weather is improving and it appears that the chance of rain is rapidly declining. At about the end of my first hour I am working up a pretty good sweat primarily because I have dressed for different weather so I stop and shed the rain jacket. I continue to see all of the same faces I have seen over the last six days and whenever we pass one another we always say the same thing..."Buen Camino". That's all you need to say. It's that simple and it matters not how many times you see the same person you always greet them the same way..."Buen Camino".

The scenery is spectacular. I will take many pictures today and they will soon be posted. The real difficulty in taking the pictures is that the more you stop to take the pictures the less you see. I know that makes no sense but it's just an opinion. I hope you enjoy some of them and perhaps match them up with something I wrote in the blog.

I am at the point where the trail begins to climb. It's long and continues to look rather easy but I soon realize that it's still a fairly long climb. It's nothing like the first very difficult days but it still gets your heart pumping. It's not boring because it's just beautiful.

As I approach the four mile mark I catch up with a young couple. I have not seen them before and something is not going well. The young woman (I'm guessing they are in their 20's.) is seriously hurting. She is limping very badly and her pace is nearly a shuffle. I stop and ask the young guy if they need help. He turns and says with a smile "thank you". That's it. She is standing still just trying to smile and I ask him if he speaks English. He nods and says yes, a little. He asks me where I am from and I tell him. I ask him the same question. He says simply "Japan ". While we are trying to connect his young companion is clearly in pain. I suggest to him that to turn back he would only need to go back about two or three miles to the nearest Albergue to get help. To continue to Los Arcos is another ten miles. He thanks me but does not comment on the suggestion of turning back. I'm not sure where they began their Camino but I think I know where it will end. I move on.

The balance of the day is fairly flat and I get to Los Arcos in about six hours. I enter Los Arcos and begin to look for my Hotel. I'm looking for The Villa De Los Arcos Hotel. It takes about ten minutes to run out of whatever is supposed to be Los Arcos. I have seen several signs pointing the way to the Albergue but no signs for The Villas De Los Arcos.

I turn back because I have run out of Los Arcos. I step into a Cafe with my iPad Mini out and fired up with the address clearly displayed in hopes that if I show a local the address they can point me in the right direction. I show the guy behind the counter my iPad mini and he looks at me like I just stepped off a space ship. As I'm trying to explain, a young woman having some power house coffee with her friends offers to help. She is an American and she speaks Spanish fluently.

She asks for a look at the iPad and begins to speak with the guy behind the counter. The guy then picks up his cell phone and calls the Hotel. The young American woman tells me that the guy has never heard of the place. That's a bit disconcerting. He ends his call and then begins to tell the young American something while pointing out the door.

She tells me that he said that the Hotel is 3 km from here and that I need to just go straight out to the street in front and just walk to where it ends and I will find the Hotel. Okay, I'm good with that. Another 1.8 miles is no big deal. It's not like I have a dinner reservation. So out I go.

I walk straight out as instructed but the street which I was simply to stay on to its end is suddenly a part of some plaza with multiple exit options. Okay, I take off my backpack to get my guide book to try and get a sense of where I am. I'm not sure but I pick a direction. I cross the street and I just know it's not right. So there I am standing in the road with my backpack on and my guidebook in hand and a Police car slowly passes by me. The two Cops in the car are clearly checking me out. I am long removed from The Camino and they know it. They move on and I'm still standing there trying to figure out where I need to go.

In about three minutes the Police car returns and pulls up next to me and stops. The cop on the passenger side says something to me in his native tongue and I respond by showing him my iPad. The driver puts on the lights and gets out of the car. The people in the bar on the corner are now very interested in what›s going on. The cop who was driving comes to me and looks at my iPad and says something to the other cop. I›m waiting. I have no clue why he put on the lights or what they are talking about.

Finally the other cop says in English that the Hotel Villa Los Arcos is 2 km away and he points in the direction I need to take. I say more than once "Gracias, Gracias". He hands me back my iPad and I am on my way!

I start walking and two minutes later they pull up next to me again and the cop in the passenger seat says "get in". He pushes open the door from the front seat and I throw my backpack, poles and my iPad into the car. I am in a Police car in Los Arcos and I don't yet know why. The cop who told me to get in says they will drive me because it will be dangerous to cross the main road to get to the Hotel. Oh good I am not under arrest!

While we are on our way to the Hotel he asks me where I'm from. I tell him "California". He turns to the driver and says something to him in Spanish, the driver responds and the only thing I pick up is "San Diego".

The cop who speaks English then says, "Aren't there a lot of people there who speak Spanish"? I answer yes. His next comment floors me. He says "then why don't you speak Spanish?" I tell him I just moved there. I just lied to a cop because I am too embarrassed to tell him the truth.

When we approach the Hotel I start to understand what they were talking about. This Hotel is basically a truck stop just off the freeway exit. They drop me off. I took a picture of the cops and after I checked in a picture of the freeway they didn't want me to navigate. I will post both. These people are just amazing!

More tomorrow. Stage 7, a short walk to Viana. It's been an interesting day. Good night.

Thursday, May 23, 2013
On my way to Viana with the Chef

You may want to get out the wine and if possible make it Italian.

The day starts with a look outside my gas station Hotel window to check the weather. It's a bit chilly and it's gray. I believe that it will rain today. I pack (including my hat) and I am ready to get a cup of some real coffee.

I did not get much sleep last night which is not all that unusual. I check in and head to my room. I am at a new and very ugly contemporary Hotel-gas station. When I get to my room I open the window. There is one giant window. It's so big that if I wanted to I could throw all of the furniture out of it and there would be room to spare.

I open the window to get some air and I start to unpack. I can hear voices, lots of voices directly beneath my garage door size window. I take a look. There are about 50 people taking a smoke break from there bus tour and the location of choice for their break is directly under my window. Okay no big deal. I can handle a little chatter if needed but I sure hope there aren't any late night bus breaks here at The Villa Los Arcos. I don't know how they came up with referring to this place as a Villa. I really don't care. I have a clean room and a shower.

Let us not forget that if not for being booked here I would not been able to take a ride in a Los Arcos squad car. That little extra was worth being in a Villa that's not a Villa.

I complete my unpacking and my preparation for my walk to Viana tomorrow. Stage 7 will be about 22.5 km or about 12 miles. What I don't know yet is that I have made an error in my travel calculations and I will soon be driving Sharel completely insane. I promise to do my best to try and make it up to her, if she is still talking to me by the time I get back.

I had no idea just how complex it is trying to figure out where and when I think I need to be for nearly 35 days. Add in all of the unknowns and the potential for weather and or injury delays and you can begin to see just how fluid this schedule might be. Throw in the fact that there is a nine hour time change and it just adds to the challenges.

I leave my room and head down to the cafeteria. I ask to see the menu and the young woman behind the counter hands me the menu and then points out that the menu items are not available until 8:00. She does let me know that I can have one of the bocadillo's out on display. That's a ham sandwich which I am beginning to believe is a staple here in Spain. I pass and retreat back to my room where I will wait for the menu items to become available. I am in need of a fork and knife required meal.

I wait until the menu launch time and return to the cafeteria. I take a seat, there are many to choose from because I am the only customer. It's a good thing I have a reservation. Because I have already gone over the menu some two hours ago I think I know what I will have. Well I'm wrong.

The head waiter (and only waiter) comes to take my order and immediately tells me "no" as he takes my menu from me. He comes back to my table and hands me the updated menu for today. The menu I had studied some two hours ago has changed. He hands me a menu which he has taken a pen to and scribbled all of the changes for tonight. I guess the "chef" is unhappy with the original offerings.

I had trouble understanding the original menu and the new hand written version is impossible to figure out. I'm in luck the misto salad is still being offered! I select that by pointing to the word "misto" and then I just take a good old fashioned guess at my main course. I point to what I'm thinking is meat. I will only need to wait a short time to find out what it is.

The waiter returns with my salad and my bottle of wine which I guess is included because I did not order it. I never had the chance when he last visited my table. The wine is not great but what can one expect. Have you ever had a great bottle of wine in a cafeteria? The salad is actually very fresh and it is surprisingly good. The loaf of bread is also good. By the way when I say loaf I mean the whole 12 inch version. They like their carbs here in Spain.

I am eating the salad as a few people who are getting gas come and go when my main course arrives. I have no idea what it is but I am sure that it's not "heart healthy". I give it a try. It's not good. I don't know what it is but I now know that tonight will be a salad night. While I am eating my salad the waiter is sitting at the counter watching some soap opera on the television and is completely into the drama. It appears that there is a wedding taking place and the bride dressed in white dramatically says no to the vows and runs off. The waiter is visibly shaken! This must be his favorite show. I can't get his attention so I go to him and ask for the check. He can't believe that I am not eating the main course and have now declined dessert, which as always is included. I need to get some sleep.

I am back in the cafeteria at 8:30 the next morning, packed and ready to go. I order my coffee and select a pastry from the two choices offered and take a seat at my favorite table. Again I am the only customer. Not for long. A guy walks in, sits at the counter and orders something and points at the pastry. The waiter hands him his selection and then pours him a glass of red wine in what looks like a small glass used for anything other than wine. Wow that's one way to get ready for the day's work. Five minutes later a second guy comes in takes a seat at the counter several seats away from the first guy, picks out a pastry and the next thing I see is the waiter giving him a real wine glass and he opens a different bottle of red wine and pours customer number two his ration of Vino Vinto. This must be the Spanish version of the breakfast of champions.

I pay the bill and go to check out. I return my key and the clerk who is checking me out has to stop the process as gasoline customers come in and ask to have X number of Euros on pump number whatever while I waiting. He takes my Visa card and swipes it six or seven times but is having a problem. He then asks me for my "secret" number. He wants my PIN number. I don't think so. I give him the 53 Euro in cash and get ready to leave. As I am putting on my backpack the manager who checked me in yesterday arrives. He sees me and comes to tell me that it is too dangerous to walk past the freeway and offers me a ride back to The Camino. These people are nice.

I believe that things happen for a reason and I am now more convinced than ever. The Police car, the Hotel location and now my ride back to The Camino will now all be a part of my meeting Michele.

I begin my 22km walk to Viana at 9:30. It's a bit chilly and it's going to rain. I am ready for it. As I prepare to start a short very stocky guy passes me. He says Buen Camino and looks at me with a look that says "wimp". I am bundled up and have even put on a pair of my extra REI socks as gloves. He is wearing shorts and a tee shirt! I start to follow him.

Less than a mile from the start I come alongside a tall guy who is also fairly young. I say Buen Camino and he responds in English and adds good morning. I ask him where he is from and he tells me Italy. We will walk the entire 22km to Viana together.

His name is Michele. He is Italian, speaks English, Italian, German and Portuguese. He is a chef, 32 years old, single and owns a restaurant in Dortmund Germany. Before I complete my story about Michele I will give you his restaurants website and I urge you to take a look. But first back to today's walk; this will be the most interesting day in my first seven by any measurement.

To start he knows everyone. As we pass others on the trail everyone shouts out his name and he enthusiastically responds in whatever language is needed. He is the Mayor of The Camino and before this day ends with dinner I will give him this title and others will begin calling him the "Mayor" of The Camino.

It's a gray day, it's drizzling and we are just on cruise control. Every now and then he will stop and with great excitement he will pick a part of a plant and stick it under my nose to smell as he describes in great detail how he would prepare fish with this plant or beef or pasta with another. I am getting a lesson in cooking and I am now schooled in the use of Latucca, Finockio and other herbs whose names I can't remember.

As we walk he becomes my photographer (photos on the way). We discuss a great deal of topics including politics, religion, food, wine and much more. He tells me why he is walking The Camino but I cannot share that with you because it is just too personal and it would be wrong to do so. Let me just say that he is walking The Camino in search of a solution to a relationship that's has disappeared and he wants back but can't figure out how to do it. He is hoping that he will find it at some point in the thirty five days on The Camino.

He knows everyone on The Camino, their names, where they are from, why they are on The Camino and more. For instance he knows Ted. Ted is the guy I wrote about from Scotland who I met in the snow storm and was wearing a kilt. Michele knows him. When he mentions Ted I tell him how I met Ted and that I took of picture for Ted and a young woman during the storm on day two. Michele immediately tells me that they are not together and that the women's name is Janet and she is an American from Indiana and that's she a writer. He goes on to tell me an incredible story which involves Janet from Indiana. Go ahead and take a sip of your Italian wine, this is good.

During the walk to Puente La Reina, Michele injured his knee and had to go to the find a Doctor to get some medical attention. His knee was badly swollen and he was in some pain. The Doctor gives him something to rub into the knee and puts a wrap on it. The Doctor also tells him that he should not walk the next day to Estella.

Michele tells me that he decided to keep going but that he hired the "donkey" service to take his backpack ahead to Estella for 7 Euro. The "donkey" service is the currier service which you may recall I labeled the "cheater's" service. He describes in great detail, how it works and that on the day he uses the service that his bag is one of about forty being taken to Estella! I knew it; I just did not know how big a business it is.

Here's the part you have the wine for. As Michele is walking to Estella, without his backpack, he catches up with a young woman who is walking alone and is struggling and in pain. He stops to ask if he can help. It's not her feet or legs; it's her shoulders that are the problem. She is carrying too much weight. He tells me that he offers to carry her backpack to Estella and she starts to cry. It's Janet from Indiana. He takes her backpack and begins to walk with her. He takes two or three steps and all of the pain in his swollen knee is gone!

He continues on to Estella carting Janet's backpack. By the way, Janet stays in Estella—her Camino is currently on hold.

There is much more to this great day which I will fill in but I am late for dinner. I am having dinner with Michele and three other Germans to whom Michele has introduced me. One of them is about my age and is on his third Camino in the last six years. I have much to learn from him and I can't wait. Tonight is going to be a fork and knife night.

Take a look. www.ristorantemichele.de

Friday, May 24, 2013
On my way to Navarette a walk of about 14 miles if you count the detour...Yes, I get lost

More about the wrong turn later. But first back to finish yesterday or my way to Viana.

Michele and are really making good time and I don't seem to be aware of the fact that it's raining. As we pass through a grove of olive trees Michele stops to show me something about one of the trees very near the path. He tells me that this tree is about three hundred years old and that at one time it was one tree but has now grown into four separate trees. He goes on to tell me that he knows this because his Father has hundreds of olive trees on his land in Sicily.

Michele gets excited when discussing olives. He shows me with his wooden walking stick how to bring down the olives in October for the pressing. He points out with great pride that the family's olive oil is the purest you can find. I ask if they produce it for sale and he says no it's just for the family and friends. His personal usage tops 50 liters a year. He likes olive oil.

Michele's Father lives half of the year in Sicily and half the year in Dortmund. He is retired and is four years older than me.

Back to the olives for a minute. As we leave this three hundred year old beauty I tell him that at one of my past homes we had olive trees brought in but we had them neutered so they would not produce the fruit. He stops dead in his tracks and just looks at me and says "olive trees without olives?" I can see him pondering this piece of info. We move on.

The balance of the day is just very simple. The landscape is spectacular and the hills are manageable. I take lots of pictures some of which I will send to Robin to attach to the blog. I don't yet know how to do it but I'm working on it. Yes, I am technically challenged, but I bet I can sell you a car if you give me a shot at it.

We arrive in Viana. We have completed stage 7 in about 6 hours including our lunch and other breaks. After checking in we agree to meet in the lounge for a beer and to meet up with the other German pilgrims.

I get my gear settled and head to the lounge. Michele is there having a coffee. The first guy through the door yells Michele's name. I am quickly introduced to Rainer who is walking The Camino for the third time. Now a second guy walks in and does the same thing. He's Big Billy. That's a name I have given him. He's six feet four and he is a big guy. Michele tells Rainer that he is still trying to get a room in Navarette. These guys have never met before The Camino and they have had dinner together every night from the start.

Rainer makes a call and with that he finds Michele a room at the Rey Sancho Hotel. Ron asks me where I am staying in Navarette and I look at my iPad and I'm staying in Najera. Rainer had completed the Camino two times so when he looks at me and shakes his head and says "no" he has my attention.

Rainer takes out his German guide book and begins turning pages and writing down some numbers. I am waiting to see where this is going. I should point out that Rainer is an aeronautical engineer so he is on this with very meticulous precision. When he completes his work he tells me that my plan will require a walk of more than 24 miles! This is a problem, a very big problem.

Just yesterday I have asked Sharel to book me out to the very end. I have decided to go straight to Santiago without a break. This can't be done with my plan to go to Najera. I need to contact Sharel immediately. She will not be happy with this little problem. In order to fix this I need to go to Navarette tomorrow and then change all of the reservations she has already made for me by one day!

I explain my dilemma to Rainer and he says quietly that if I want to keep my schedule I should consider taking the bus to Logrono which will cut off seven miles leaving me with about 17 to Najera. The bus is not an option. That would be far worse than using the donkey service. I can see that he likes my response to the bus idea. He's just trying to help.

I fire up my iPad and send the dreaded email to both Robin and Sharel. I flinch when I hit the send button. It's about six thirty in the morning in California. This will not be a good way to start her day.

They get it done! Robin sends me an email that tells me I am confirmed at the Rey Sancho Hotel and Sharel has already fixed the next three days after Navarette. No excuses, I just miscalculated the miles and that's as simply an explanation I can give.

Michele makes the dinner reservation for five people but there are only four of us. The fifth dinner guest is not yet here but I will meet her at 7:30.

Its 7:30 and I head back down to the dining room where all have gathered and I meet our fifth person. Her name is not Sofia but that's what I am going to call her until I can find out her real name. I am introduced to her as she sits across the table from me. It's noisy in the restaurant and I can't hear so I just let it go. I will find out her real name later.

Sofia is17 years old and is walking The Camino alone. She can't possibly weigh 90 pounds and Big Billy tells me that she is carrying 23 pounds! That is insane. The target number is ten percent of your body weight. Sofia is carrying more than double that. Rainer just stares ahead and says nothing. I think I can read his mind. There is a long way to go.

I ask how her parents felt about this idea and she tells us that her Mother was in favor but her Father is not. Her mother walked The Camino and believes it is safe.

Let me not forget that at this table for five everyone speaks at least two languages. All four speak perfect English. I am the only one who speaks only one language. I'm getting use to this but it's not making me feel any better.

While we are on the subject of backpacks and weight I ask Big Billy if he's heard about Michele's encounter with Janet from Indiana. He's not being argumentative but he responds very quickly. I should note here that when I ask the question I don't yet know that Big Billy has had dinner every night with Michele.

Big Billy turns to me and says with a great big smile on his face that "yes I have heard the story". He looks at Michele and says, "It was the medicine, a bandage and a good Doctor". He turns and smiles at Michele. I'm waiting for Michele to say something. He turns and looks at me and says "Jim knows, right Jim?" My response to Michele is yes. I turn to Big Billy and simply say "it had nothing to do with medicine". Michele is just smiling. I think they have had this conversation before. The topic of weight is revisited.

We look at the menu and I decide to start with a little pasta, which turns out be very good. For my main course I go outside the box and order the Rabbit. I've never had Rabbit so why not. The waitress is now bringing out our main course and she hands me the fish. Everyone has their food and all of their orders are correct because no one is looking to send anything back. I keep quiet; I don't want to delay the dinner.

It turns out that the fish was excellent and it has with it roasted peppers. The wine is local, Rioja, it's very good and very reasonably priced. I am about to begin but first Michele hands me the olive oil. I put a little on the peppers and it works.

I will stop now and head to dinner. I will fill in some blanks as best I can. It was a late night. Tonight will be a very early. I will cover stage 8 which was today's walk to Navarette later. I need to eat.

Friday, May 24, 2013
Dinner goes late...Very late and long after desert

I've got one final note about dinner in Viana with my new German friends. When we order dinner we are asked to select all three courses when the waitress takes the order. I guess you could ask for a delay of your desert selection until after having the main course, but it just doesn't work that way here, so you just go with the system and get with the program.

I order "fruit" as my desert menu selection. I have now finished devouring my Rabbit, which comes from the ocean. I actually ordered the Rabbit but she brought me the fish. I could have sent it back but I really don't want to be the ugly American. I will just eat it. The waitress also brings me my desert choice, the "fruit". It's a fairly large plate and on it is an orange. That's it, an orange. I watch the waitress coming toward me and it's amusing to watch her trying her best to keep the giant object from rolling off the plate. When I say giant object I am talking about a very large orange. My orange does come with something else, a knife, a very sharp knife. This is another reminder that I am in Spain, not Capistrano.

We now retreat to the "Salon" aka the living room for our nightcap. I stick with the wine but everyone else is having the coffee. Not the con-leche version, they are all having the high-test version. I don't know how they can sleep after the coffee. I know that I'm not having any. The night goes long, the topics are many. I lose track of the time and before I realize it it's 2:00 am when we finally head to our rooms! This cannot become the norm. This cannot be done even one more time unless it happens in Santiago when the journey is complete.

Because I am now going to Navarette and not to my original much longer destination I can sleep in and all will be good. Meeting Rainer was a blessing and it results in getting my schedule in order.

I leave Viana at 10:45. On my way now to Navarette--stage 8--a walk of about 12 miles. I pack and head to the front desk to check out. I am leaving the room and I just have this uneasy feeling that I am missing something or leaving something behind. I am correct. My walking poles are missing. They are not in the room. It would be hard not to find them if they were in the room. By the way I look at my critical list and I don't have them listed. How could you lose your poles? I will just have to deal with it.

I am at the front desk paying my bill when I look down in the corner of the reception desk, and there are my poles leaning against the wall exactly where I left them while checking in yesterday. I make a mental note to make a change to my list. I don't have my one pair of shoes on the list either but I'm starting to think I should include them. With me anything is possible.

I will walk alone today. Everyone leaves when it best suits their desired pace and the length of the day's scheduled walk. It's just the way it is. I'm sure I must be the last one out.

It is about 7 miles from Viana to Logrono, a large city with a population of more than a quarter of a million. I think that's right. As always, before I leave my room, I open the window to get a sense of the weather. It's sunny and cool. Perfect. I dress for what looks like a nice day.

I leave the hotel and within ten minutes I am cold, just pain cold. It's sunny but it's cool and the wind is up. I stop at the first spot where I can deal with the wardrobe change with my backpack on a wall or something. It just makes the process of getting things in and out of the bag a lot easier. I add my fleece vest and will now have on four layers. I also put on my REI gloves (socks) and as I am going through the change, a young guy passes me wearing shorts and a tee shirt. He gives me the look as he says "Buen Camino". If he has a blog it probably describes him passing the old wimp with the white beard wearing the socks on his hands. What a wimp.

Yes the white beard. More about that at another time.

I head to Logrono having not yet eaten anything. I am starting late and will just wait until I reach the city. I make fairly good time and for the first time I would describe the scenery as not worthy of stopping to take any pictures. Most of the next seven miles is on small paved roads with very little traffic, almost none.

I am passing through some less than upscale neighborhoods which just remind me that I am close to a large city. As I make my way around a right hand turn down a little hill I get my first glimpse of the dogs, lots of dogs. There are about seven or eight of them, they are all barking at me and they are all small except one. The big one looks like a shepherd and his bark indicates that he is not happy to see me. I have read about the wild dogs in more than one book while getting ready for The Camino. What I have read is correct. This is where you are happy you have your poles.

I am about fifty feet from the big one; he has not yet started toward me like all of his little friends. The little ones are of no concern they are just running around me making all kinds of noise. I'm waiting, but the last thing I want to do is stop and give the big one a sense that he is in control.

I'm now getting very close hugging the opposite side of the path from him when he jumps in my direction and then I see it. He's on a chain big enough to tow a truck! His chain keeps him at least ten feet from me as I pass him. I yearn for the quiet part of The Camino.

Entering the city I am getting concerned with how few signs and markers there are for The Camino. The city is noisy, lots of traffic and lots of people to get around. I am hungry and need my coffee con-leche.

It will take nearly an hour to get through the city to get back to The Camino. I stop at the Royal Cafe. Pastry and coffee, two cups, they are small and I am good to go. Before I return to The Camino I need to find an ATM. I don't need any more cash but I'm not sure that once I leave Logrono I will be back in the smaller villages without ATMs where cash is the only method of payment. I find one easily. I leave the city and I am making good time. No aches and pains, all good. My training is paying off and it's also given me a new appreciation for what Robin goes through when she trains for a marathon. She has completed three marathons. She ran the New York marathon twice and last year she ran the Chicago marathon in addition to a number of 5 and 10 K events. She put in lots of hard work and many hours of preparation. She is probably running at the beach as I write this. You go girl!

Speaking of writing, I received an email before I started today from Pat. He and seven other guys from the Club are in Florida playing golf. I was invited but I'm a little busy this weekend. Thanks Billy for the invite--sorry I could not make it. I am sure that there will be some good wine and at night a little four on four Ginn game.

I can just see it now. Paul is playing Bobby and says "how can you take that card?" At which point Bobby knocks and gets 45 points. Paul is a Golf Professional, a Touring Professional, currently out with an injury. He is the better golfer but Bobby is the better Gin player.

I mention Paul and wonder if he is reading my blog and grading it. He is a former school teacher and I expect that when I get back and see him at the Club, he will give me my grade. Hopefully, he grades on a curve.

Please keep in mind that when I write my ramblings each day I am often tired and I will make spelling and others errors, it's been a while since I wrote anything more than a short email. I try to edit them as best I can but you will just have to bare with me. Or is it bear with me?

Once out of the city I will have about 5 miles to go. Well that's what I am supposed to have remaining. I am now stopping to drink some water, sit for a minute or two, and go through my third wardrobe change of the day. It's gone from being cold and windy to warm. I'm down to less than two layers and the sock gloves are long gone. I'm not sure what the temperature is but when I was in the city a bank's temperature and time sign said it was +13. I'm guessing it's about 60 degrees.

I leave for what should be my last two miles and I should arrive in Navarette at about 4:00. I cross over this bridge where a dozen or so old men are fishing and make a left and continue on the trail. I walk for about twenty minutes and realize that I have not seen a single Camino marker. That's odd. I walk another ten minutes and I see a sigh for a golf course. I stop and take out my map. There is no golf course on my map. There is a large regional park which The Camino passes near but does not go through. I am clearly in the park. I turn around and double back to where I made the left turn. There was one yellow arrow (the standard color for The Camino) at the turn but I just missed it. I have added about two miles. I knew this would happen I just hope I don't make it a habit.

I arrive in Navarette and find my Hotel, the Rey Sancho. When I enter the lobby there is no one at the front desk and it's dark. In most of these small villages the lights in most rooms are triggered by movement. Leave the room and soon after the lights go out automatically until someone steps back in. This makes sense. I trigger the lights and I see that on the front desk there is a bell, a really large bell. I wait and then take a guess. Am I supposed to ring the bell for service? I give it a try. Wow, this is a serious bell and when I ring it I'm sure that everyone in town knows that there is someone at the front desk of the Rey Sancho who wants to check in.

Soon after the bell stops ringing a young woman checks me in and hands me the remote for the television in my room and politely reminds me that I need to return it when I check out. I'm not sure why I bother to take the remote, there is absolutely nothing I would want to watch and it's all in Spanish.

I take care of my gear, take a shower and head out to get something to eat. There is an outdoor cafe fifty feet from the Hotel. I take a seat and soon after I am having a slice (it's actually square) of pizza and a glass of red wine. When finished I head back to the Rey Sancho and call it a night. Its 7:15, perfect.

I get a message from Michele that he and he and Rainer will be in the restaurant at 7:30 if I want to join them. If not coffee in the morning before we all leave for Najera a walk of only about 10 miles. A short day and I'm looking forward to it. Good night.

Saturday, May 25, 2013
The Vineyards of Rioja

I get to sleep early and I wake up early but I am not tired. Today I will walk to Najera through the Vineyards of the region, Rioja.

Today's blog will most likely be shorter than the others are because the trip is only 10 miles. When I reach Najera I will be about 124 miles into this journey. I was thinking about this on the way today. With the completion of my walk tomorrow I will have walked the equivalent of a walk to south San Diego and back. I can't help it; it's what you do when you're walking for four hours.

I pack and as always I take a look outside. The sun is out and it looks like it will be a good day. I head down to the lobby and give the desk clerk my key. He smiles and just says "television". I forgot to bring the remote back to the front desk.

For those of you keeping score this error with the remote does not count in my "I lost this something score sheet". Having just used the word "lose" (as in lose my phone) correctly for the first time since I started this blog instead of "loose" (as in my pants are loose) demonstrates the comment I made yesterday about my errors in writing the blog. While I am at it, from now on my "poles" will describe my walking tools and they will no longer be referred to as my "polls", as in an election. Corrections and editorial work is ongoing but I can still feel my grade declining.

I return the remote and go directly to the coffee and bread feast in the small dining area. The couple from Brazil is there and they immediately greet me with "Buenos Dias!" I have met them once at dinner in Viana. They came to our table to say hello to "The Mayor". They are the nicest people. I have also passed them on the trail and they always say "Buen Camino" regardless of the number of times you see them. They smile at all times.

I order my coffee and orange juice. The desk clerk also takes care of the dining room. I watch as he prepares the freshly squeezed orange juice. He brings it in a pitcher. It's delicious. I wonder what The Four Seasons would charge for a pitcher of freshly squeezed OJ? Mine is included with my room. The room charge is 48 Euro or about $65.

My coffee arrives at about the same time as Rainer. We start with the all-important tropic, the weather. Rainier has already completed the research and tells me that it will be cold today probably a high of 10 C. Shortly after, both Michele and Big Billy arrive. I am surprised to see Big Billy because the last time I saw him in Viana he was thinking about staying an extra night because of the blisters on his feet. He tells me that he has decided to deal with the blisters and stay on the same schedule.

Rainer then mentions the treatment that is best including not putting anything on the blisters and especially don't wash your socks. That comment about the socks gets my attention because of my daily laundry habits including the washing of my socks. I ask why? Rainer points out that the more often the socks are washed the more quickly they will lose their shape. In addition the thickness will also be reduced from multiple washing which results in a different fit in your shoes. If the fit you have is working don't change it, simply stop washing them as often. Rainer is on his third Camino; my socks will no longer be a part of my daily Tide event.

Soon it's time to go and we all head out. I fall behind quickly because when we leave I am cold. The wind is up and it gets my attention quickly. I stop to add a layer and to get my REI gloves out as well. Within less than a minute or two I am passed by a guy with shorts and a tee shirt on. There must be somebody arranging this daily event designed to make me look like a wimp and working, but I don't care because I'm cold.

Within a half an hour I catch up with the Michele, Big Billy and Rainer. We share a couple of words and I move past them. My pace is well ahead of theirs. It may be related to Big Billy's blisters. There is no violation by me moving on since everyone just goes at their own pace. It's also better because if I join up they will be nice enough to switch to English for my benefit. Without me they can all stay in their native tongue, German.

I catch up with and pass the Brazilian couple and as always they are smiling and greet me with the customary Buen Camino. They left the Hotel well ahead of me so I am making good time. I'm not pushing it but the trail is flat and the temperature is perfect for walking. I am on a pace that is working for me.

There is only one hill of any size and it's a three stager. It's not that steep, but there are lots of rocks and boulders and damage from the recent rains so I just take it slow.

As I reach the top I turn into another vineyard. The entire 4.5 miles will be right through the vineyards. I reach a point on the trail where there is a small group of buildings and the trail splits very dramatically into a choice of very left or very right. I stop and search for a Camino marker when a small tractor working in the field close by beeps its horn. I look over and the driver has his hand out the window pointing to the right telling me which way to go. I avoid a detour and wave at him with my poles and he beeps back again and waves goodbye. These people are nice.

I have gone so quickly that I miss the tiny village I was going to meet Michele, Rainer and Big Billy in for coffee. I just go right past it. The next thing I know I am in a much larger town. As I cross a river on a bridge older than anyone I know I am not sure where I am. Is this the small village which Rainer described as the place where we would meet for coffee? I don't think so. As I reach the end of the bridge I spot a guy I have seen on The Camino a number of times before. We have always given each other the standard Camino greeting but I have never spoken with him. He is no doubt an American. I greet him again and after I move past him I stop and turn back and ask him if he knows how far it is to Najera? He is standing there looking at the same guide book I have in my backpack when he responds. "This is Najera". I am stunned. I am here in less than four and a half hours and I stopped for a couple of breaks. I tell him that I was thinking there were about two miles to go and I ask him where he is from. His name is Jerry and he is from Massachusetts and I immediately let him know that I grew up in Connecticut and that I have been a Redsox fan for 50 years. We are now bonded.

We chat for a short time but long enough to find out that his brother lives in Bakersfield California and that he has very bad blisters because he did not train and has the wrong shoes. We wish each other well and he moves on.

I am in Najera and I am well ahead of schedule. Now all I need to do is find the Hostal Hispano and I will get settled and take a break. The weather is so good that I am looking forward to dumping all of my stuff and having a coffee by the river.

Najera is small and quaint to say the least. I find the Hostal in less than ten minutes. The difference between a Hostal and a Hotel is primarily the ownership structure and the amenities offered. The Hostal's front door is locked and there is a sign telling anyone with a reservation who arrives before 4:00 pm to go to the bar around the corner to check in. That's another difference between a Hostal and a Hotel.

I follow the instructions and when I walk into the bar I am greeted by a baby who cannot be a year old in one of those round things that lets them move around like they are walking when they are not. I've seen these before. As I walk in everyone stops what they are doing and stares at the old guy with the white beard, backpack, and poles and shouts some kind of collective greeting. I feel like I just returned for the family reunion!

I am offered food, wine, beer and of course everyone speaks perfect English. Sharel has put me into this great little place in a perfect location with these really nice people and it costs about $60. I like Spain.

I take care of my gear, take a shower and decide that I will chill out and catch up on some reading. Ten minutes into that idea I am sound asleep. I wake up at 5:15. I will take a walk and try to find my German comrades. There are only three Hotels in Najera and they all sit on the riverbank. I step outside and it is beautiful, about 65 degrees with the sun shining. I think I will go find a seat at an outdoor cafe on the river and just take it all in. I see this as a bonus from The Camino for past which was very hard.

I am looking for a spot to sit and sure enough Rainer is at a table by himself having a glass of wine. The next two hours with Rainer are very interesting.

Rainer is an aeronautical engineer employed by a very large international airline. He has been with them for almost 40 years and will retire in two years. As noted before this is his third Camino. I ask him why he did the first and he tells me that he still does not know. Perhaps it was the challenge? He says yes, maybe. Rainer is a very intelligent man. When we had coffee this morning he had a long conversation with the desk clerk in perfect Spanish so that puts him in the three language group: German, Spanish and English.

I ask him about the second Camino and he says he still does not have an answer. I don›t ask him about the third Camino which we are now on. It just does not seem right to pursue the topic.

He goes on to tell me about a small part of The Camino's history including a great story about a very wealthy French women and The Camino. I will try to get it straight.

There was a French woman who was poor before she walked The Camino. Sometime after her Camino experience her fortunes changed for the better and she became a very wealthy woman. As she grew older she called in all of her children who were all estranged from each other to tell them how each of them could get their share or get nothing, the rule was that in order to inherit their share of her fortune they would all have to walk The Camino together. Each one who completed The Camino as a part of the group would receive their share.

The story goes on about how walking together heals their personal wounds and they complete the Camino together fully reunited.

Rainer is currently carrying four stones from friends who have asked him to place their stones at a specific place. The stones from each person have their own meaning and purpose. I don't think there is any doubt that there is a spiritual purpose to the four stones. If you have seen the movie The Way you will recall the placing of the stones.

I am with Rainer one on one for the next two hours before we meet Michele for dinner. Big Billy is busy holding a table for more than three hours in order to secure a good spot from which to watch the European equivalent to our Super Bowl, the European Soccer Championship. This year for the first time there are two German Clubs in the final. One of them is Dortmund where both Michele and Big Billy live. This is a really big deal. Big Billy has brought with him his yellow Dortmund shirt to wear at the restaurant. By the way Big Billy's real name is Christopher, but I like Big Billy better so for my blog he will remain known as Big Billy—my privilege.

Michele, Rainer and I go next door to have dinner while Billy holds down the table. The restaurant/bar has already told him that he would need to order food for the table of empty chairs at least twice before the big game starts. Just in case you were not aware the other team is Munich.

How about this. There are 22,000 seats available in a lottery for the game. More than 500,000 are in the lottery and I am sitting with Big Billy who has one of the 22,000 seats. He proudly shows me his ticket on his iPhone. Its value on a system like eBay is more than 5,000 Euro or nearly $7000 dollars. I ask him what he did with the ticket and he tells me that he gave it to a friend in London. By the way the game is being played in London.

Michele, Rainer and I finish our three course dinner including tax, tip and wine, a cost of about $15 each and go next door to be with Bill Billy for the start of the game. I took a picture of Big Billy in his yellow Dortmund shirt which I sent to Robin.

The game starts and the place is packed. Soccer is big here and the European Championship attracts even those who don't care just like the Superbowl. In the first ten minutes the action is slow and very defensive but suddenly Dortmund has a great opportunity to score but just misses. Big Billy jumps up when his team misses the great opportunity to score taking with him all of the beer and anything else on the table. No problem. When Big Billy stands up and starts to clean up the mess no one would be dumb enough to tell Billy "down in front".

I leave at half time while 99% of the fans step outside to smoke and no one will know that I am gone. Tomorrow The Camino takes me Santo Domingo a trip of about 14 miles. I need the rest far more than I need to see the end of the game.

Good night.

Sunday, May 26, 2013
Munich 2, Dortmund 1...Big Billy is not happy

I head back to my Hostal Hispano well before my German friends will get to bed. Big Billy is to put it mildly very engaged in the game. Sitting at the very next table is a Munich fan who is nearly the same size as Big Billy. I had a feeling before I left at half time that these two very big guys both so completely committed to their teams may end up facing off.

I am not proud to tell you this, but I have been in a couple of bars before and I know what can happen when you get this mixture of emotions and beer thrown together and it's not good. I will tell you more about the end of the Big Game later.

I am back to the Hostal by 9:30. I am the oldest in the group by a stretch and I know how I need to feel at 7:00 in the morning if I am about to throw on a twenty two pound backpack and go for a 15 mile walk. Watching Dortmund and Munich does not fit into a solid plan to make stage 10 painless. I get a decent night's sleep and leave the Hostal at 8:45. I need to return the key and my remote to the bar across the street because the actual front desk in the Hostal building is not occupied until 4:00pm. I don't care where I return the Hostal's property I just want to have a cup of coffee and perhaps something to eat.

The woman tending the bar is very nice and greets me in nearly perfect English. I give her the key and the remote and she asks me if I would like a cup of coffee? Yes, con leche please. As she prepares the coffee she asks "would like something to eat?" I take a shot and ask if it would be possible to have eggs? She turns toward a little room in the back which I cannot see into and begins speaking to someone in Spanish.

A voice from the little room fires back and the young woman says to me "Mama wants to know if you want scrambled eggs or an omelet with cheese and ham?" I choose the omelet. Good decision. I am about half way through the omelet when Mama steps out from the back. She takes one look at me and turns to her daughter and in Spanish asks her a question. The daughter then tells me that Mama wants to know if you are tired. All I say is "no". After more conversation finally the daughter tells me that Mama says my eyes are tired and that I need more sleep. No argument here. It's just not that simple.

I pay the bill, 53 Euros (about $65) for room, breakfast with tax and tip included. Try that in Capistrano.

I thank the daughter and put on my backpack and I am on my way to Santo Domingo De Calzada, fifteen miles away. Today is stage ten so it's my tenth consecutive day of walking. I am averaging just about 15 miles a day and I am grateful that I don't have any serious aches and pains.

I will soon find out just how much better I am doing than some of the other Pilgrims I have met along the way.

I am starting to understand that when I first start each day I am a bit sore and yes a bit tired but soon thereafter things get better. Once I have walked about a mile and a half my muscles warm up and I get more and more comfortable. It's all about the pace and of course it also depends on the weather and the condition of the trail.

Today is just perfect. Not a cloud in the sky and a little chill in the air but without any significant wind. This is about as good as it gets for walking 15 miles.

I am walking alone. My German friends have probably stayed out well past my bedtime and may be getting a later start. All three of them are staying at a Hotel not far from my Hostal. Before I left the game we confirmed that we are all staying at the same Hotel and agree that will meet for dinner in Santo Domingo.

After about three miles it gets a bit warmer and I have already worked up a pretty good sweat so I stop for a wardrobe adjustment and a little water. I am in no rush. The walk thus far has had only one hill challenge. I have my secret weapon and the hill is not a match. I take it without stopping. I am not trying to prove anything and I am in no hurry. It just happens.

The scenery is once again spectacular. The mountains I am marching toward are covered in snow and I am surrounded by vineyards in every direction. I am still in the Rioja region. That will soon end.

I take a couple of pictures and as I do I can hear a group of voices getting closer. It's a group of seven locals out to walk to the next small village about a half mile away. I guess that's what they are doing because they have no poles and no backpacks. I don't like having people directly behind me so I decide to take a short break.

I wait to let them get well enough ahead and as I begin to get back on the trail Michele walks up beside me. He is all smiles and asks if I want to walk along with him. Yes, absolutely and we move on. Our pace quickly matches the same pace we used when we first met leaving Los Arcos. The conversation quickly turns to how fantastic the weather is today.

Before I left Najera I did not think to ask anyone at the Hostal if they knew what the result was of the Big Game last night so my first question to Michele is "who won?" He stops and tells me the story about how in the final minute of the game Munich scored the winning goal. Munich 2, Dortmund 1. He says something about it was not a good ending and goes on to tell me just how upset Big Billy was and how the subsequent face off with the other big guy nearly caused a riot. No punches thrown but it got close and the people in the bar made sure they were separated. Big Billy is so upset that he tells Michele and Rainer that he does not want to talk to anyone and leaves.

In addition to Big Billy's disappointment with the game he is also still struggling with blisters and has decided to take the bus to a Burgos which is 4 stages away. That will cut off about 60 miles from the total. Big Billy is the first victim I hear about today but he won't be the only one.

Michele and I are making good time. I am twice his age so I think I am doing fairly well. I feel good and I am telling myself that I am walking for the tenth consecutive day and I don't have any issues which will slow me down. I don't want to jinx myself but I am beginning to believe I can complete The Camino without stopping. It's now my goal.

There is one very long hill that stretches for about a mile. It's a gradual climb and it's long and over some poor terrain. We take it slow. Shortly after reaching the top we see a small village ahead and we agree that we will stop for coffee and a small bite of something.

The name of the village is Azofra. We stop and take a table outside at the Bar Sevilla Azorfa.

We are drinking our coffee and diet cokes when a young and very small woman spots Michele and shouts out his name. It's amazing, he knows everybody. It turns out that this young woman was part of a large dinner group with Michele in St Jean at the start of The Camino. He has not seen her since. Her name is Mee-Sue (that's how she pronounced it) she is from South Korea and she has hurt her knee. Michele takes out of his backpack the bandage he used back on the way to Estella.

He tells her to sit and he tries to get the bandage around her knee but she is so small that it just keeps wrapping around making the Velcro useless. He makes a comment about how small her legs are and she responds that he has the legs of an elephant, it's pretty funny and Mee-Sue is pleased with her ability to make a funny comment.

Michele decides that he can turn the bandage a certain way and tie it which he try's and it works. Mee-Sue is better and gets back on the trail ahead of us. We will see her again.

As we get started again we can see off in the distance some very dark clouds and we are walking directly toward them. We are about 5 miles from our destination. Nothing is said but I know what I'm thinking.

As we get closer we turn through a small village which has all of these very modern, very ugly and completely abandoned groups of apartment buildings probably a result of the global downturn back in 2008. They don't look like they will be occupied any time soon.

Just as we come around the corner someone yells out Michele's name. It's the Brazilian couple I have seen every day at many of the Hotels and every day on The Camino. They immediately break into Portuguese and we decide to join them for a short break. Michele introduces me to them, Fernando and Nelly. They are from San Paolo and they are the nicest and happiest people on The Camino. They are discussing Hotels which need to be booked and Nelly (who speaks English) is looking for Hotels in all of the cities ahead of us for the next ten days. I take out my iPad mini and show Nelly the schedule which Sharel has put together for me and she is ecstatic. She asks if I can email it to her when we reach Santo Domingo and of course I say "yes". Sharel, Nelly and Ferdinand both send their thanks!

We finish our break and we need to get moving the storm is getting closer. We are only two miles away from completing the days walk. Our pace is much faster than our friends from Brazil and they are soon well behind us. In the end we all make it to the hotel just before it starts to rain. Well almost all of us. We have passed Mee-Sue down a very long hill which takes you into the city. She is struggling; the effects of the bandage have worn off. She will soon be wet as well as in some pain. The Camino has another victim.

Michele and I have not seen Rainer today and when Michele left his Hotel this morning Rainer was still in his room. We both think that Rainer is probably out on the trail getting wet. We are wrong. Rainer walks up to us and says that he's been waiting for us. How is that possible? Simple, he took the bus! Too much wine watching the game and then he stayed out later than planned. When he woke this morning he was just not up to it so he took the bus.

That's okay. Rainer has completed two Camino's, he is allowed the use of a donkey or the bus. It's time to head for dinner. Tomorrow I will go on to Belorado, 14.2 miles away. The forecast is not good so let's keep our fingers crossed.

Monday, May 27, 2013

I'm not a good tourist...The Church with the two chickens...

It's 6:30 in the morning, it's Monday May 27th. I just wrote that just to try and keep track of the days. It's been two weeks since I flew to Madrid. Today will be stage 11 a walk to Belorado of 14.2 miles.

I know nothing about Belorado and I doubt I will see much of it when I get there. I just looked out the window, it's raining and it's a steady rain. Aside from the rain, the desire to get out of all the wet gear and chill out will have no impact on my desire to be a tourist. It's just not me.

I am sure that Robin, my brother Rick and sister-in-law Jill can attest to that. We have traveled to many great cities in some of the most beautiful parts of the world and I have seen little. I just don't like getting on a bus and having some guy who does not know how to use a microphone with the volume out of control starting every sentence with "Ladies and Gentlemen, Ladies and Gentlemen" over and over again. That actually did happen and I nearly lost my mind. I can see the three of them now as they remember the number of times I would just say no thank you to joining them on some excursion to who knows where to see who knows what. They are also smiling right now saying a collective "thank God!" I would be a real PITA and just make them all crazy if I came along. Being a tourist is just not my thing, it has its draw backs.

Case in point: After last night's dinner with Rainer and Michele we step out the front door to check on the weather. It's raining and the forecast is for rain all day. This is a beautiful little town and Rainer points to a church next to our hotel and asks if I have gone in? No I have not. When we first arrived today I was focused on getting into the Hotel lobby before it started raining, so when I passed the Church I really didn't notice it. It's beautiful. My lack of tourist skills are sharp.

Rainer asks if I know the story about this Church and the two chickens. Of course not, I live less than a mile from The Mission of San Juan Capistrano, one of the oldest Missions in Southern California and famous because it is where the swallows return each year to the Mission after flying thousands of miles from South America. I no practically nothing about this Church I can walk to from home, how would I know anything about a Church half way around the world in a place called Santo Domingo, population 5600?

Here's the story. I will do my best to get it right.

Legend has it that hundreds of years ago that a couple walking The Camino with their son stop at an inn on their way to Santiago. While there they visit the inn and the owner's young daughter is attracted to the young man but he is not attracted to her. The parents return to The Camino, the son will soon follow.

The young girl angry that the young man has shown no interest in her falsely accuses him of stealing silver from the Inn. He is arrested, convicted and hanged.

The parents become concerned that he has not been seen so they return to Santo Domingo to search for him. They find him still hanging from the gallows but still alive thanks to the intervention of Santo Domingo. They rush to the sheriff's home where he is about to have his dinner. They tell the sheriff to release their son but the sheriff responds by telling the parents that it is not possible because their son is as dead as the chicken he is about to eat, whereupon the chicken stands up in his plate an crows loudly. The sheriff understands this to be a miracle and rushes to the gallows to cut down the young man and he is given a full pardon.

The family then continues its journey on The Camino to Santiago.

There were so many miracles, accredited to Santo Domingo that the town takes his name. To this day in the Cathedral of Santa Iglesias there are at all times two chickens in a coop above the alter. Two new chickens occupy the coop every day, including today.

The Church of the two Chickens. I will wait as long as it takes to enter the Church before I leave to see the two chickens, I don't care how long I have to wait. I am going to visit the Santa Iglesias Cathedral.

At 9:25 this morning I enter the Cathedral, it is spectacular. A building you would have to see to believe. That it can exist in a town of only 2600 is truly amazing. I go to the alter and there they are, the two chickens. I took a picture but flash is not allowed but I think you can see the two chickens. Robin will post the picture among others for stage 11.

I am going to be a tourist today. I am seeing a lot along the way but much is being missed. I will try to be better at being a tourist but still no buses!

Get your favorite glass of whatever that happens to be, because this is not believable.

I have breakfast with Rainer it is about 9:00 am. It is raining and there appears to be little chance that it will stop anytime soon. I am prepared. I have on extra layers because it is chilly and I also have on my rain pants. They are very uncomfortable. Warm and difficult to walk in, this is not a good combination for a 15 mile walk in the rain.

I visit the Church of the Miracle of The Chickens. I see the two chickens and then go back to the Hotel. By the way there are about 18 chickens selected for this honor and the two selected are changed each day.

Michele has joined Rainer and me late for breakfast and decides that he too will visit the Cathedral to see the chickens. When he returns it is already 10:15 and it is still raining. We cannot find Rainer. Michele calls Rainer's room but there is no answer. Perhaps he has gone ahead, we don't know. We make a decision and we leave for the Camino thinking that Rainer is ahead of us, regardless we leave. It's 10:30 in Santo Domingo.

The walk today is fairly easy. I can't believe that I just said that. Today is my eleventh consecutive day and I just said "fairly easy". I need to be careful not to get ahead of myself. I still have a long way to go, a very long way to go.

As we leave the town it is raining lightly but I am at the point where rain just does not get my attention like it would if I were home. It's laughable when I think of how my friends and I would react if we had a light shower surprise us while playing golf. Immediately there is a flurry of activity while everyone puts on their rain gear, grabs the giant umbrella and begins protecting the towels needed to wipe down the seats of our covered golf carts! Something tells me that I will see rain differently when I play again.

Michele and I am only a bit more than a mile or so from our start and I am sweating like someone about to testify at a murder trial. The sky in the distance is blue and it appears we are headed in its direction. We stop to take off a layer.

I shed both a vest and my rain jacket. Why not, the rain jacket is as wet inside as it is on the outside. Ten minutes after taking off the rain jacket it starts raining again. I'm not going through another change, I will just get wet.

We are really moving along, the terrain is flat and the light rain has softened the trail making the walk more comfortable on my feet. My Limos are performing well. I check my watch and I estimate that at the pace we have been moving that we have already covered a distance of about four miles. We will stop at the next village for coffee and a bite to eat.

As we enter the village it's a common theme. It's a small village with a giant church. If you could see these buildings it would make you shake your head at not just the size but the architecture. I know someone who would take far more time to look more closely at what I am just dashing by. Gene will enjoy the pictures.

As we approach the small bar/cafe Michele makes a small detour for the Farmacia. He wants to buy some ibuprofen. I mention that I will need to by some eye drops. He asks what I mean and in order to explain I just pull back an eyelid and say "too much wine". He laughs and now understands. It's not the reason I need the drops it's just that the weather and the wind keep making my eyes water and yet they are dry. I can't explain it.

We are in the Farmacia and Michele is speaking with the woman at the counter. She is explaining what dosage he should take. I only know this because I hear her say "dos", two. My Spanish is very poor but I can count to ten.

It's my turn and Michele is explaining what I need. She turns to me and I just take a piece of paper and write down Vispring. I bought these before in Pamplona. It works. We are out the door and on our way to have our coffee.

I have my coffee con-leche and Michele has his straight. There is a selection of small freshly made bocadillo's (sandwiches) and we decide to share one. The bartender cuts it in half. The meat is a very tender ham with cheese and tomatoes. As always the bread is just so much better than anything I could get at home.

As we are having our sandwich I can't help but think of my brother-in-law, David who passed away far too soon. He would just love the food here. I miss David. He was fun to be around and I really enjoyed eating with him. He appreciated good food and he knew how to eat good food. David could sit with a small plate of cheese, olives, olive oil, Italian bread, a few slices of pastrami, and a small glass of wine and take an hour to eat it. When I ate with him I would slow down and enjoy the food. I miss him as do so many others.

I continue to be amazed at how little I am eating in spite of the energy I am burning on The Camino. Smaller portions and very few snacks in between and yet I am not hungry. The one exception is dinner. By the time I arrive at the destination of the day I am ready to eat. Today will be no exception.

As we leave the village there is a small dog just ahead and Michele stops to remove something from his backpack to offer the animal. He kneels and speaks to the dog in Spanish. The dog is very jumpy and Michele explains that all of the dogs here are afraid perhaps because of their lack of care. He tosses the snack to the dog. He takes it and with that two other dogs are jogging toward us. Michele offers both a treat and the big one, who appears to be blind in one eye takes the treat directly from his hand. As we walk away I ask him what it was he was giving them. They are long, thin, and dark and look like sticks. They are dog treats he has brought from home. He tells me that he has a dog at home, Jessy, and that he misses him and asks if I have a dog. "No but we do have Vivian El Gato de Interior", the house cat. He remembers, I showed him the picture Robin sent me and laughs as he repeats her name "Vivian, Vivian".

As always we leave the village and pass by two pilgrims I have not seen before and without hesitation they call out his name and he responds in German and they both laugh and wish us Buen Camino. The Mayor is gathering votes. He could win in a landslide.

As we make our way toward Belorado it is sunny and it's getting very warm. I could be wearing shorts today. Yes even the wimp from California can handle this temperature. It's really a nice day. We joke about it but I have told Michele that he is lucky to walk with me because I am blessed and he will reap the benefit of my good fortunes and have great weather. He repeats "Jim is blessed" as he gestures toward the blue sky. It just keeps getting better.

We have not seen many of the usual group of Pilgrims today; perhaps it's because of our late start. We continue on. There has been only one small but long hill. The heat from my rain pants is increasing but I am not going to stop and take them off, it's just too big a hassle and if I do take them off where will I put them? They are covered in mud and will make a mess of anything in the backpack.

We are moving at a pace that is much faster than in days past but we are not pushing it. It just happens. We see a sign for Belorado telling us that we are about six miles away as we leave the Rioja region. More of the signs I see make reference to Santiago still hundreds of miles away but it's a solid indication that I am getting closer with each step. Twenty three more stages after today, only twenty three.

There is one point in today's walk where we both stop and think that we have missed a turn. We have walked at least two miles from where a sign had indicated that our Hotel was a short 3km away. This is troublesome. There are no Pilgrims in sight in front of us or behind. The trail in front is long and we cannot see anything that looks like a village. For a moment we both realize that we may have to turn back and repeat a couple of miles. Not good.

We are standing there and I spot a stone in the grass and sure enough it is marked with The Camino shell. We have not made a mistake so we press on.

Michele is starting to feel some discomfort in his shoes. He tells me that he decided to turn over his insoles that morning and that is now proving to be a mistake. I myself have two small blisters, one on a toe on my right foot and one on the heel of my left. No point in dwelling on it. They will need to be dealt with when we arrive.

As we enter the village it's no different than most. Big Church, small village but this church is different. On the top of the Church there are very large bird nests—very large, enormous. Michele stops and asks me the name of a very big bird and I say eagle or hawk. He thinks and then says no, the bird that brings the baby. A stork—they are everywhere.

We turn the corner and there are three people sitting on the ground and they all shout out "Michele". I am introduced to everyone as "Jim from California". Edward is sketching the church and is very talented. We agree to meet later in the plaza.

We reach our Hotel and agree to meet between 6:30 and 7:00 for dinner. Rainer has not yet arrived. I guess he did not start ahead of us.

Once the gear is cleaned and taken care of it leaves some time to rest. I make a note that I am nearly out of the Tide packets Robin gave me so I will need to find a market soon.

I head downstairs and Rainer and Michele are already there. Rainer knows a good restaurant but first we will take a look at two others. We settle on the first choice and take a table for four. There is no one else in the place. There is a television mounted on the wall near us and Michele asks if it can be turned off or at least reduce the volume. The woman working the counter looks less than happy but manages a smile. Little do we know that in just ten minutes the television volume will not matter.

I order a salad and a steak. The steaks in Spain are razor thin not at all like the 24 or 26 once choices we have at home. Before we finish the salad about 15 very loud old guys show up and sit right next to us for their card game. We can't hear anything. Asking for the television volume to be turned down in this place is silly.

Once we pay the bill we head for the plaza. We meet up with Edward, his brother Kevin, the woman from Australia and a college student from Texas. The conversation starts out like most conversations among pilgrims meeting for the first time. Everyone has met before but not Rainer and me.

Among the typical questions: "Where are you from?", "Where did you start The Camino?" "Are you going all the way to Santiago?" And more.

Edward and Michele ask Kevin to play something on his guitar. I have never seen a guitar as small as this guitar. I have no idea what to expect. He begins to play and I realize that I am watching a very talented professional musician. He is so good that the locals start to gather. Kevin had once lived in Spain for ten years. His Spanish is perfect. Not good, not great, perfect. As he begins to sing in Spanish the crowd begins to grow. It's a show as Kevin serenades a couple of the old women. They are singing along. He is very, very talented. His is a professional and it shows. Soon there is a local who is speaking to Kevin and that results in Kevin handing Alberto (I know his name because the locals are encouraging him to play) which he does and he is good but the unique guitar is not his cup of tea.

I took video of the performance. I wish I could share it with you.

Kevin is back playing when Alberto returns with his Spanish guitar and the two play a duet that I will not soon forget. It's great entertainment. I have met a number of really nice people on this journey but none nicer than Kevin and his brother Edward.

They are returning to the States tomorrow after spending 12 days together. One brother lives on the east coast and one brother lives on the west coast. I know what that's like.

I need to get to bed, tomorrow is a walk of 15 miles to San Juan de Ortega and it includes an elevation increase of 1200 feet. As much as I would like stay I am not willing to pay the price for it tomorrow. I go back to the Hotel. Good night.

Wednesday, May 29, 2013
Suan Juan de Ortega...A village so small it has only eight Hotel rooms, Sharel gets me one!

I don't know why but I am just not organized this morning. I did get a good night's sleep but I'm just not with it. I will be walking to San Juan de Ortega today and I just realized that I live in San Juan Capistrano and the main road into town is Ortega Highway. That's odd.

As I pack I realize that there are two items missing. A pair of socks I left on a window sill after washing them and a pair of sunglasses. I admit to this for those of you keeping score. Most of my friends are probably impressed that I made it through two weeks without losing anything. Just a reminder, for those of you who took the under it's time to collect your bets.

I meet Michele and Rainer at the combination bar, lobby and breakfast room. I could just have a carb overdose but instead I choose a small sandwich to go along with my cafe-con leche. I like the con- leche but this beard is becoming a problem. My con-leche is sticking to my mustache and its bugging me. I will try to trim it when I get to San Juan.

I'm sure you are probably sick of the weather report but here it is. When I looked out the window this morning it was raining and dark.

Sound familiar? I will dress accordingly but I am not going to wear the rain pants. They are just too warm and very uncomfortable. I will just get wet. I may leave them behind and reduce weight. I'm not sure.

As we are having our breakfast Rainer tells me that he will only be going as far as Villa Franca De Oca which is about 6 miles from Belorado. Rainer wants to check out a highly rated Hotel there and in addition he cannot find a place to stay in San Juan.

Michele also is without a room and there is little chance of that changing. There are only eight rooms in San Juan de Ortega and according to my guide book the population is twenty. This San Juan is much smaller than the one I know. I wonder how big its Church will be.

To walk 15 miles and not have a place to stay is not a good idea. Michele decides to join Rainer at the new Hotel in Villa Franca.

It is 10:15 and I have a tough day ahead so I need to leave. Rainer says he will wait a while longer to allow for the rain to pass. I won't see him at the end of today but we will have dinner on Wednesday night in Burgos. Michele is thinking about going on and taking his chances. In order to really have that as an option he knows he will need to leave with me now.

It's chilly but a great temperature for walking. We get started and are soon facing some nasty mud. All this rain has now turned parts of The Camino into a clay-based, deep, thick mud which is difficult to get through. Today will be a day when your poles will give you a return on your investment. I hope my Limos are up to the challenge.

The Limos can at least look forward to a good cleaning when we arrive in San Juan.

You may be asking yourself, what does he use to clean the Limos each day?

I read a book or a blog about preparing for The Camino and it had a great tip which I paid attention to. The author suggested bringing a small micro-fiber towel. Only a bit larger than a foot square but capable of handling any dirt and so easily washed out and very fast drying. Let us not forget one other benefit of this simple towel, it weighs next to nothing. After that day in the snow with my Limos soaked and covered in mud this little towel got them ready for the next day's challenge. The little towel is now on my critical list.

The rain is light and on and off, mostly off. I have removed my rain jacket, it's getting warmer. I think that I may change when I climb to the higher elevation which lies ahead. Once again our time is good. The conversation is good but occasional. As we approach a long stretch of mud which covers The Camino completely it becomes a kind of dance. You are looking ahead and down trying to pick out the best route through in order to avoid a deep pocket which would suck the shoe right off of your foot. Having wet feet for another ten miles is not something I want to experience again. I go slowly while up ahead Michele is just plowing his way through.

It does not take long for us to have a gap between us of several hundred feet. We walk at our own pace and that's the way it must be. It's unspoken. We will catch up at some point ahead of us and if we don't that is fine.

Keep your own pace and listen to what your body is telling you. If I had a critical list for the walking The Camino this rule would be first on the list.

Once we are through the larger mud holes the trail returns to normal. Michele is still ahead but I am closing the gap. He is walking with someone and their pace is slower. I catch them. Michele introduces me to this woman I have not seen before on The Camino. Even Michele has not met her before. They are carrying on a conversation in French. Yes, French.

Michele is interpreting and he tells me that she started her Camino in Leon. That's odd; Leon is ahead of us several days away. He explains. The woman who I would guess is older than I am has started her journey from Lyon France! She will walk 52 days to Santiago a distance of more than 750 miles. Incredible.

Her pace is slower so we wish her Buen Camino and head off.

There is a small village a short distance from where we are and decide that it will be a good place to stop for coffee. I estimate that we have gone only about 3 miles. The mud is slowing the pace. We enter the village and just arriving at the cafe ahead of us are Fernando and Nelly. We exchange greetings, handshakes and hugs all around.

Like all of the other tiny little cafes it has the usual selection of topas and snacks. We all order coffee in the way we prefer and take a seat. Fernando and Michele are debating who has the best coffee, Italy or Brazil? Fernando tells me that in Brazil some people put Coke in their coffee! There are some things I am willing to try. Putting Coke in my coffee is not going to make that list.

As we get ready to go Nelly wants to check my list of reservations which Sharel has worked so hard on putting together. I know Shrael would not mind, she would love Nelly.

I am looking for the correct email and I can't help myself as I scroll my inbox. I stop to show Nelly a picture of my Grandsons. She loves the picture and makes several comments in Portuguese which she then tells me in English, "They have your eyes". Yes they do I just hope they are not looking as tired as mine.

The next thing you know we are looking at pictures of their two beautiful daughters ages 20 and 22 and their two tiny dogs which are completely dressed in their fancy little outfits looking like they are about to walk in a parade. Miss Vivian makes an appearance and then we must leave.

The break went long and I still have about another eleven miles to go. Michele and I are quickly well ahead of our Brazilian friends. More mud ahead and we are once again separated by pace. The weather remains good with a great temperature for walking or for riding a bike. There are many who complete their Camino journey on bikes. I don't envy them.

Most of the people on bikes have bells on their bikes to ring and warn you that they are rapidly approaching from the rear. On occasion they will not warn you and suddenly they fly past you usually in a group. They can really startle you, but worse, with no warning you could take a step right in their path as you try to avoid an obstacle on the trail or inadvertently get a pole out in front of them as they pass which could result in something very serious.

There are times when they just fly by me as I am walking down a steep hill where I might envy them but uphill in the mud, I will take my Limos anytime.

As I approach the village of Villa Franca I can see Michele ahead talking with someone on the trail. I catch up to them and It is an older German woman we have met before, they are discussing accommodations or the lack there of. I am now about 9 miles from my destination and I say goodbye. I will walk the last 9 miles alone. I will meet Rainer and Michele in Burgos for dinner. We are all staying at the same Hotel.

Once I am past Villa Franca the walk gets significantly more difficult. I am now facing the 1200 foot climb and there is mud, lots of mud. There is no way to take this hill on directly. No, this hill will require several stops and a fuel break. It's warm and I will need to keep a pace which reduces my risk of overheating. As it turns out today will be the first time I will reach my destination for the day and enter the village out of water.

I take a couple of pictures, one looking back down the hill covering what is past and one in front which I will call reaching the top. Good idea except this is not the top. There is a short flat section above but shortly after another hill, the last piece of the elevation.

I walk for at least seven miles without seeing another pilgrim in either direction. As I stop for a little water I can see ahead a real problem. So far I have been able to dance my way around, over and through the mud but what I am now looking at is mud that is much thicker and there is plenty of deep water. There are no options you just do it.

This patch of the trail which is a completely muddy mess continues on for about a half mile. It is really slow trying to pick the best of the sections to try to get past. Finally I am out of it. My feet are fine and they are dry. My poles have once again proven their value.

Suddenly I can see the village of San Juan de Ortega. It will not be difficult to find the eight room Hotel in this village. There are only two sizable buildings: the Church and the Hotel. I go directly to the Hotel and find a sign instructing me to go to the Marabell bar to register. I can see it; it's only about a hundred yards away. The process is quick. There is however no food available until 7:00. I order a diet Coke and a small bag of chips. That's all they have.

I return to the hotel and begin working on the gear and the mud. By the time I have it done and shower I am ready to return to the bar to check out the menu. While there I ask about Wi-Fi. The guy at the bar just says no and then he points just outside the door to a tiny building that looks like a storage shed. Inside there are two coin operated desk top computers to access the Internet. I throw a bunch of coins in and it tells me that I have purchased 26 minutes of time.

I begin. 21 minutes into the process I am not any closer to sending an email as I am to a great restaurant. All of the instructions are in Spanish. I keep seeing Google and I just keep guessing and suddenly it's in English and I am in. I send a short email to Robin telling her that I have made it to San Juan and that there is no Wi-Fi so no way to download both blogs for stages 11 and 12. That will be the cause of my posting delay.

The dinner will be a Pilgrims dinner in a very crowded little room with food I don't want to eat. I buy another bag of chips and a glass of red wine and head back to my room to enjoy my gourmet meal and get some rest. I will eat tomorrow.

Stage 13 tomorrow 15.4 miles to Burgos. Good night.

Good night.

Wednesday, May 29, 2013
I am hungry and I don't want to talk about the weather.... The weather girl does not like me.

I will complete my 13th day today on The Camino. This is stage 13; I am on my way to Burgos a walk of 15.9 miles which I will turn into at least 17 miles. No, I did not get lost, I will explain later. Before I post stage 13, I would like to catch up on a few items which I have either discussed before or did not include in a prior post that may be of interest.

A quick update on the Camino missing in action. It›s day 13 of the journey and I have not seen Mee-Sue since Michele put a bandage on her knee. I don›t think she is ahead of us.

The 17 year old girl who I gave the name Sofia to is doing fine. We saw her at our free outdoor concert with Kevin and Edward in Belorado. She is safe and walking with a group of people who are younger and moving at a very aggressive pace. Sofia (I actually know her real name but I will just call her Sofia) has reduced the weight of her backpack by getting rid of several books and will leave The Camino in the next two days to return to school. I give her a lot of credit for her courage for what she has done but I agree with her Father— I would have said no.

Big Billy is somewhere up ahead and I may see him again. I hope so; Big Billy is a gentle giant that you would all like to be around as long as Dortmund is not getting beat. Hopefully his feet are better.

Janet from Indiana has not been seen for several days. She may just be lagging behind after a rest or she may have ended her Camino in Estrella.

The young Japanese couple I met several days ago when she could hardly walk is most likely gone. Her injury just appeared to be too serious to consider going on. The Camino has no limits on injury. Young and Old will be tested.

Jerry from Boston is healing his blisters and will be leaving The Camino in the morning. His plan is to return to the Camino this summer to complete the walk. He plans to break-in his new shoes long before he returns good idea.

Fernando and Nelly are here in Burgos but Nelly is having some problems. I know it's not uncommon to have an injury end your Camino long before Santiago but I hope they will be with me there on June 19th when I enter the Cathedral of Saint James. I hope that she gets to complete The Camino If that's what she wants to do.

Now on to stage 13, San Juan De Ortega to Burgos.

I am no longer concerned with my Camino grade. I have decided on a new grading system. I will use the grades given to me by three teachers not just one. Paul will continue to grade me just like the East German Judge grades the US diver in the Olympics, you know 6.5 out of a possible 10. That's okay because I have decided to appoint as the other two giving me a grade on my Camino blog two recently retired teachers, my brother Rick and my sister-in-law Jill.

I am now no longer concerned with having to repeat The Camino based on one very tough teacher's grading process. One last comment on my most recent blogs: I have really tried to edit them as best I can but the combination of typing on my iPad mini, the size of my fingers and the fact that I am tired is just making it difficult. Sorry.

It is 8:30 and I am in no hurry to leave but I want out of this eight room village. I am just waiting for it to warm up just a little. It is cold. Not chilly, it's cold. Here's what I am facing today. A nearly 16 mile walk, at least two very steep hills and then as it turns out I will enter the city of Burgos and take the wrong route, there are two. That is where the extra mile will come from. If I could read a map better I could have avoided this but I think it's just a reminder of how spoiled I am because of the GPS woman who is somewhere hiding in my dashboard. You know her; she's the one who says "in 200 feet make a legal U turn!" I don't like her.

This blog will need to be finished later. I returned to the Hotel after dinner with Rainer and Michele later than expected. More on that soon but just a short comment it's really great having your own guide and as I suspected the choice of restaurant was terrific. In addition there will likely be limited Wi-Fi at our next stop. Oh by the way here in Spain it's pronounced we-fee.

Here is how it starts. I return my key to the combination front desk, bar, and potato chip restaurant. I will have a coffee before I go. There are none of the usual carb choices. I have not had any real food for 24 hours and that was a small bocadillo. It's cold. I'm about to find out just how cold. In walks this young woman, probably in or just out of college. I will soon give her the name "weather girl".

I am just finishing my coffee when she walks in. I say "Hola" and she responds in English "it's cold, really really cold". She continues, "its minus 1", "it's really, cold", really cold ".

I know it's cold and I know why she is "really, really cold". She is dressed like she on the way to Nordstrom's to buy a different pair of running shoes from the ones she is wearing. "May I join you?"

Yes but I'm just finishing my coffee and I need to get out of this place to walk about two miles in search of something to eat so I am not going to sit here for another twenty minutes while she drinks her coffee. I am also getting a vibe that she may be looking for a walking companion. That's not going to happen. I have no interest in having her join me. I don't know her pace, I don't want to wait and I have no interest in getting a weather update every fifty feet. I'm out of here.

The next village is Ages is small but bigger than San Juan, which does not make Ages unique. I pass the first cafe. I don't know why given my interest in getting something to eat. It turns out to be a good decision. I spot the next cafe, it's fifty feet away. I go in and I am blown away at just how beautiful this little place is. I have sent pictures which I hope Robin will post.

The cafe is spotless. The woman behind the counter greets me like I am her favorite son just returning from war. I am the only customer. The meat and cheese choices are extensive. I don't know how this place can survive.

I order a coffee-con leche and she says "grande?" Sure why not. As I drink my coffee she is creating a bocadillo which has two types of ham which she slices as thin as you can imagine and adds cheese, tomato and drizzles a bit of olive oil, adds salt and pepper and I am in heaven.

The bocadillo is also made with the bread she has just removed from her oven. It is so big that I will eat only half and have the rest for lunch. I also buy a bottle of juice and a small bar of dark Swiss chocolate, an energy boost. I pay the 5 Euro, thank her and I'm on my way.

I have been there for about 30 minutes. I step outside and who do I see? It's the weather girl. I greet her "Hola" and she stares at me says nothing and gives me a look like I have insulted her. I have now officially made my first enemy on The Camino. You can imagine how bad I feel. If you can you have me confused with someone else. I could care less.

I have learned many things in walking nearly 179 miles about The Camino rules, one of which is if I want to walk alone for whatever reason you must respect that wish and move on. She knows about as much about Camino rules as she dies about footwear.

I am also sending now a picture of my next car. I spotted it on the way out of Ages. It's a beauty. It has a spoiler so it must be fast! I'm not sure about the color I will order but I know it won't be red—I already own a red car. Robin will post the picture. You will be jealous.

That's it for now. I need to get the Limos on and get back on The Camino. Have a good day and to all my friends playing in the Dove Member Guest, "hit it where they mow."

Friday, May 31, 2013
Bethany Shea...1942—2012

This is the continuation of my walk from San Juan de Ortega to Burgos. I am leaving the "village *of* 8 rooms" and a population of 20 to walk 15.9 miles to the city of Burgos with a population of 166,000—quite a contrast. There will be one very significant elevation change along the way and nearly half the distance will be on paved roads as I approach the City.

The weather girl was correct, it's cold and the wind is blowing at about 20 miles per hour. If she really wants to be a weather girl she should also include in her summary a wind chill factor.

The Camino leaving Ages is very similar in its terrain until I am facing the hill. It's nothing but rocks. Rocks of all shapes and sizes and none of the trail has been spared, I will have no dance moves which will help me avoid this challenge. My Limos and poles are veterans and ready to go.

The climb is made slower by the wind. Its direction is directly into me, a head win. Several stops to complete the climb are needed. No hurry, avoiding mistakes that would turn an ankle are far more important than speed.

As I reach the half way point I can see the Cross at the top of the hill. I can also see the large collection if rocks at its base. I won't know how tall it is or the size and number of rocks until I reach the top.

When I finally reach the top I can now see just how large it is. The rocks have been placed there by pilgrims at the base of The Cross. The pilgrims have also left behind other personal items.

I begin to see items just beneath the rocks. Notes and pictures many impossible to see completely because of the rock cover. I am about to turn away and get back to The Camino when I look down one more time and there it is.

Almost as if it was meant to be seen by me, there is one picture beneath the rocks which is completely visible—a picture of a woman looking right at me. It has on it above her picture only her name

Beverly Shea and just beneath her picture the dates 1942—2012. It's a nice picture and she looks like a nice person. Someone close to her has placed it here beneath The Cross. A message to that person or persons: The picture is still in good condition and she looks happy.

The Camino on its way to Burgos is different from many other parts I have walked since I started in St. Jean. Until now the villages were separated by significant distances. Today they are much closer together and they appear to be more in need of repair. Perhaps it's the City effect. The Closer you get to the City the closer all of its typical problems become exposed. I don't know maybe I'm just reading too much into it.

At about nine miles the Camino changes from trail to pavement at in increasing rate. Traffic and noise are the norm. This has been by far the least attractive walk. With about three or four miles to go I am walking along a very narrow strip of pavement facing the rushing traffic which are now primarily trucks, very big trucks. I feel like I'm walking toward Newark New Jersey on I-95. There won't be many pictures taken today.

I am now entering the outer fringes of the city so I decide to stop and take a look at my map. The last big city I entered was Longrono and getting through it was a real challenge.

I am looking at the map and its shows two Camino routes into the city from where I am. The primary route is always marked in yellow and the alternate route is marked in green. I have been walking for 14 days on the yellow route, I'm not about to change.

For the next two hours I am walking through some rundown industrial area that is a mixture of ugly buildings sprinkled in between some really ugly buildings! If this two hour walk is representative of what Burgos is I will be looking forward to tomorrow's exit.

I am finally in the part of the city which helps me to immediately forget the last two hours. It's very beautiful. The Cathedral of Burgos is stunning and it is big. Pictures once again begin making sense. My only problem is that I'm no closer to figuring out where my hotel is now than I was two hours ago. I know I have walked well past 15 miles.

As I am wandering through small side streets trying to find the Feran Gonzalez Boutique Hotel I nearly step on an old lady who is sitting on the ground surrounded by all of her worldly positions and holding a small wooden bowl.

I solve my Pamplona error and she is stunned by what I place in her bowl. She is thanking me continuously as I walk away. Finally the better ending I referred to back on stage four or five. I'm tired and I take a seat in the Plaza Of Santa Maria. I am reading my guide book and map when an older Spanish gentleman asks "where are you going?"

I show him the map and he politely tells me that I am a good distance from my Hotel and shows me how many turns I will need to make successfully in order to find my Hotel. He pauses, points and says "taxi". These people are nice and they are smart too.

I find the taxi stand drop my backpack into the trunk and I am in the taxi for about 15 minutes. There would have been no way for me to have found this location to say nothing of the fact that I had walked past my destination by about a mile and a half.

I am tired and I need to find a Supermercado to pick up a few things. First I will check in and rest for a few minutes. As I check in the desk clerk hands me a note about meeting Michele and Rainer for dinner at 7:00. I don't have much time so the rest will need to be put off.

I need to stop today's post and get my shopping taken care of then take a shower and have dinner. I will catch up tomorrow from here and then it's on to stage 15, a nice walk of 13 miles from Burgos to Horrnillos del Camino.

Good night.

Friday, May 31, 2013
Dinner and a Bull fight....It's not much of a fight and it sure isn't fair.

I run out from my Hotel here in Burgos having completed stage 15, I need to get a few things, I am out of Tide. Can't believe I just wrote that but it's true. My focus on The Camino is very different from what I would normally be concerned with if I were back in Capistrano.

I find the Supermercado a short distance from the Hotel. There is nothing "Super" about it. We are so spoiled. This "Super" market is not as large as the wine and deli sections of our "Super" markets at home. If the people who are in this market right now could just see what the difference is I doubt they would believe it.

I don't find any Tide packets but I do see a box of powered detergent that has on its cover a picture of clothing items being washed by hand? It's called Veep. I will buy it. The box is much too big but that's not a problem, I will just poor some of it into a zip lock bag and leave the rest behind.

I go back to the Hotel and take a quick shower.

By the way now is as good a time as any to get this on the record. I have lost my second pair of sun glasses. For those of you keeping score I believe that's item number three. Update your records.

I meet Michele and Rainer in the lobby at 7:00. Rainer will lead the way to a restaurant he has been to before. I know it will be good because Rainer has taste. He takes us through a stunning part of the city past the Cathedral de Santa Marie built in the 13th century and then over the river past the most famous stature in the city. It's the statue of El Cid, born in 1040. His house is not far and The Camino passes close by. Can you say tourist?

We arrive at the restaurant, Don Jamon. As Rainer has already explained there will not be any pilgrims here, it's strictly locals. We will feast on a continuing selection of Tapas. The food is just as good as I knew it would be and the wine is even better.

When we arrived in Burgos we entered a new wine region. We are no longer in Rioja; we are now in the Ribera wine region. Rainer orders a bottle of T-Danguix. I think it was 2009, not sure but I can tell you that it was very good. Hard to believe that it costs about $14 US! Keep in mind that's the restaurant price.

Now for the hard part about dinner—we are in a favorite local restaurant and on one of its walls facing our table directly is a very large flat screen television, probably the sixty or seventy inch variety, and for as long as we are there the Bull fights are on.

I understand that Bull fighting has a long history in Spain and that the people watch it with great passion. I am watching and also getting an education on what is taking place. The patrons at the bar and in the restaurant are cheering and I am told with the introduction of each bull there is great and very animated debate about the "quality" of the Bull. As each Bull is brought into the arena where some 20,000 people are watching live the details on each Bull is scrolling across the screen. The Bull's name, his owner and his age and weight are for all to see. The first Bull I see on the screen weighs 1200 pounds and as I learn quickly he had no chance of winning the "fight", none.

What the patrons are debating is if the Bull is fast enough, angry enough and willing to make the Matadors have to work hard to kill him. There are as many as six Matadors surrounding the Bull when he is finally dead, but during the "fight" there is one primary Matador who everyone will be cheering for. He is a rock star.

I watch only one event in spite of the fact that while I am sitting there at least ten Bulls are tortured and put to death. I am certain I will never watch a Bull "fight" again.

We finish dinner and the bill is about $18 US each, wine, food tax and tip included. The Bull fighting front row seat was free, no charge.

We are on are way back to the Hotel and Rainer makes sure we return by a different route in order to see a little more of the city.

The weather is perfect and walking is not a problem for any of us. I think you can understand why.

We stop at a small cafe, bar and Rainer orders three coffee drinks called Cararrio. I have no idea how to spell it but it's a very small espresso with a touch of brandy. Hard to believe but it actually helps get you to sleep. I can't explain it, you know the coffee part.

While we are there Michele spots something he wants to try—olives with small pieces of sardines in olive oil. I try the olives and they are very good. I pass on the sardines, but Rainer and Michele will not let them go to waste.

We head back to the Hotel. It's 11:00. There is plenty of time for a good night's rest. We agree to meet for breakfast at or around 9:30. Tomorrow will be stage 15, a walk of 13 miles to Hornillos del Camino.

Before I sign off I want to tell you that I am trying my best not to over use words or word combinations like amazing, unbelievable, beautiful, fantastic, nicest, spectacular, unforgettable and many others. It's just not easy. I trust you will cut me some slack. I know two teachers who will. Good night.

Friday, May 31, 2013
The smallest room I have ever stayed in....

My change in expectations makes it very comfortable. It's Thursday the 30th of May and this will be my 14th consecutive day of walking The Camino. I feel really good, stronger actually. I know how silly that may sound but it is true. That does not mean I can explain it. There is something that does help me get started each day: Messages from friends and family that I read before I dress and pack for that day's walk.

Each day has one thing in common. I know that I have never seen or been in all of the places I will walk through today. It will all be new and therefore a bit more interesting but also a bit more worrisome.

After I wake and before I begin packing I will look at my email. It's my connection to the people I care most about. I got off to a good start today.

My day started with a terrific message from Tony Baloney (it's what I call him) a friend I have come to know over the past seven years because we are connected by a friend, Big Johnny 1438 from Scottsdale. Thank you Tony, you have no idea how much your message helped me get started today.

The weather looks very good and when I open my window I can feel a bit of a chill. This is a great walking temperature. I completed my packing and have added a few small items like the laundry powder which adds a little weight. That's okay because I have decided that I will also leave the rain pants behind. All in all I think it's about even resulting in no change in the weight of my backpack.

I arrive at the breakfast room and Michele is there just getting started. Today's offerings include the usual carb choices but today we also have scrambled eggs and fruit. I will have a little of everything along with orange juice and my cafe-con leche.

As we start eating we both find it odd that Rainer is not there. Normally he is the first to breakfast but not today. When thirty minutes pass Michele decides to call his room. No answer. A visit to the front desk and we are told that he has already checked out.

It's a bit odd because he said 9:30 and if he decided to go early, which is fine, we both would guess that he would have left us a message. We wait a little longer but decide at 10:30 we must leave.

The walk out of the city is much better than my entrance route. We walk through Santa Maria square past the Cathedral and we are shortly on The Camino. The distance between Burgos and our destination, Hornillos del Camino will be 13 miles and it will be flat.

Unlike other segments, today's walk will have very few potential places to stop for coffee along the way. We will stop in Tarjados but that can certainly change depending on a variety of things.

Our pace is fast. Yes, fast. The trail is flat and the sun is warm. There is a breeze with a temperature I'm guessing of about 60 degrees. We will soon stop to make wardrobe changes. I will take off the rain jacket and at first it will be a little cold. It won't take long for that to change at the pace we are moving at right now.

I stop on occasion to take a picture which creates a gap between Michele and I. Camino rules, not a problem. As I close the gap with Michele I can see ahead two people sitting, taking a break. Michele is talking with them and starts to move again just before I arrive. It's the Weather Girl!

The Weather Girl has found a young guy to walk with. She has one of her Nike running shoes off and as I past them she is on her feet being helped by her walking partner. She has her arm around his shoulder as he tries to help her put back on the shoe. Just ahead is a long downhill section which will require the use of poles which will cause them a problem.

As I walk past them at a good pace I know she recognizes me but says nothing. Just think that could have been me! Sometimes I make good decisions.

I am soon alongside Michele again and we agree that we have covered about six miles. We approach a small town, nothing unusual and as we turn near the end of the town we are greeted by "Michele Michele", Fernando and Nelly. They call us to join them for coffee and we do. Margaret the older, small German lady is there as well as Anna from Brazil. The first time I met Anna a couple of days ago I think I may have referred to her as French.

Coffee and a Coke Zero, a few pictures with everyone's camera and a cookie from Fernando's endless stash and Michele and I are on our way. The Brazilians started their walk today at least an hour and a half ahead of us and we are now in front of them. We will see them at the end of the day.

The walk is uneventful and we arrive in Hornillos del Camino at about 3:30. Actually Michele was ahead of me by about twenty minutes because of my camera work.

I walk into this very small village and enter the cafe and I am greeted by a loud collective "Jim, Jim from California" from Michele, Emma, Emily and Elaine. Michele is holding court and is also busy trying to find a room. There are none in the village not even in the Albergue. Rainer is not in the village and has not been seen.

There is a bottle of wine that the girls have purchased for three Euros which is about $4 US, retail. I pass and order a small beer on tap. The counter guy asks if there is anyone named Michele. Yes and Michele is now in a conversation and gathering information.

As it turns out Rainer did leave early and is staying in a Hotel that is about two miles off The Camino and he has secured a room for Michele. The Hotel will send a van at 5:30 to pick him up and take him to this offsite location. Michele is very happy and decides to buy a very nice bottle of wine at a cost of ten Euro which we will all drink while waiting for the van.

Michele's transfer is similar to what happened to me in Los Arcos but my transfer was in a Police car— far more interesting.

The van arrives and Michele is off. The pilgrim's dinner is in just fifteen minutes so I will just stay and have dinner and then head back to my Hotel.

There are five of us for dinner—Me, Nelly, Fernando, Emma and Emily. Emily is a physical therapist working in a hospital in Sweden age 26, Emma age 27, is thinking about work or school.

Emma tells us all that it's her Father's birthday. I can see what Nelly is thinking as she interrupts for Fernando. There isn't any Internet service or Wi-Fi but there is a phone booth. I can't remember when I last saw a phone booth. I ask Emma if she is going to call her Father. She then decides to call and asks if we will all get in the booth to sing Happy Birthday to him. Everyone agrees, yes we will do it.

Emma calls but her Father is not home but will be back in ten minutes. False alarm as our salads arrives. As we finish the salads Emma tries again and yes he is there. She waves us to get into the booth as she speaks with her Father in Swedish.

On cue, we all begin singing Happy Birthday to Emma's Father—Nelly and Fernando in Portuguese, Emma and Emily in Swedish and me in English. When it comes time in the song to inject the person's name none of us know what to call him so it just gets garbled. We finish the song and there is loud applause from all of the other pilgrims just sitting down to eat. I think Emma is happy that she decided to call. I know Nelly is.

Dinner is over and I head back to my Hotel to take care of the gear and to complete some writing. It is 7:30 so an early night, perfect.

I enter my room and it is really small. I have to turn sideways to get past the end of the bed in order to get to the bathroom. The bed fills nearly all of the room. It's at this point that I realize that I don't care. It's clean and I am tired.

I decide to take inventory of all of the things I would ordinarily expect in a Hotel room which I now don't find all that important. Here is what I could think of. I'm sure I missed a couple of things.

My little room does not have, a phone, soap, shampoo, a shower cap, conditioner, a closet, a mini-bar, glasses, a cork screw, room service, more than one light, an extra towel, an iron or an ironing board, a television, a radio, a wakeup call service, a bathtub, a scale, a night stand, a cable guide, a high end shopping guide, an extra pillow, a free tooth brush, a ceiling fan run by remote control, a do not disturb sign to hang on the door, a patio, an ashtray, free bottled water, a coffee maker, carpeting, a chair, a sofa, a table, pen and paper with the Hotel's logo, a free post card, a comb or brush, a hair dryer, a thermostat, Wi-Fi, a Bible, hangers, slippers and last but not least a turn down service.

I'm sure I have over looked a number of other things I would normally expect to find in my Hotel room. Perhaps you can think of something I missed.

I'm tired, good night.

Saturday, June 1, 2013

It's Friday May 31st, on my way to Castrojeriz. Thirteen miles, we will lose a regular to an injury.

I made an error in a prior post by referring in it to Stage 15. That's was wrong, today is stage 15. This is my fifteenth consecutive day walking the Camino. Sorry about that. It's difficult to keep track of the days. I am sure that I have sent pictures to Robin with a note about the picture and have used the wrong stage number. Sorry Honey, I will try harder.

I leave my little room and first I have coffee and a single piece of toast. That's all that is offered. No problem I will get something on the way.

The weather is once again very nice. It's May the 31st as I mentioned. It's a big day back at Dove. The Member Guest is under way and I can only imagine what is going on.

First I will guess that there is lots of talk about some guest who showed up with a 13 handicap and shot 74 on the first day! People are always upset when this happens. Several guests are calling home having flown in from out of state only to realize that the member can't read his own greens asking himself why did I say "yes"?

That's ok, by Saturday there will be a long list of members telling their guests to look around or just take a picture because you will never see this place again! Oh I do love the Member Guest. My brother and I will be there next year. Book it.

The landscape is not all that different from the last few days. Michele, Rainer and I all leave Horrnillos Del Camino together but that won't last long. Pictures and pace will decide that and I walk about half of this stage alone. The gap between the three of us changes constantly. At times I am with Michele and at times I am with Rainer.

I would guess that we are about three miles into the walk and Rainer and I are together when we catch up with the older German woman, Margaret. She is not well. We stop and Rainer who is also German begins to ask questions. She pulls up her pant leg and it's not good. Her left leg from the ankle to the knee is swollen badly and it's is covered in what looks like a rash.

She goes on to explain to Rainer that she had surgery on her left foot in February and again in March. Something is very wrong and while I'm no doctor the surgery comment and what her left leg looks like makes me believe there is a connection.

She tries to convince Rainer that it's probably just a reaction to the bandage she had been using. I doubt that but I keep quiet as Rainer talks to her about where the next Doctor will be and that she should consider using a donkey service to get there. The conversation ends, she says she is fine and we leave. We have ten miles to go.

Rainer, the Camino veteran tells me that the next stop is only about two miles. There will not be another opportunity to stop until we get to the final destination for today.

As we approach and then enter this very pretty little village we turn up the hill and everyone we have been with on The Camino from St Jean is sitting at tables outside having something to eat and drink. It's like a reunion.

Elaine, Emma, Emily, Michele, Nelly, Fernando and even Mee-Sue have made it back. Everyone accept Margaret. A couple of new faces from Ireland are also part of the group but I have not met them yet.

We leave together but are soon walking alone. I like the solitude. It causes you to think of many things that will surprise you when they pop into your head. Here is a great example and it's one that will cause me to keep a smile on my face for the next mile at a minimum.

I am walking along and have blocked out the fact that in this stretch of The Camino no matter where

I look I see those ugly wind turbines everywhere, and then I remember something really great because of the turbines.

Back in the mid-eighties I went to northern California to conduct some due diligence on a wind Energy Company that wanted to raise money from investors in order to build out their wind project and grow the business.

My job was to help determine if the project was a worthy investment. I represented the third party marketing firm which would take the idea to Wall Street firms which could then offer the idea to qualified investors.

I returned from my visit and brought with me all of the Company's offering materials which included a video tape presentation from a senior member of the management team. So there I am on a Sunday afternoon watching this fairly short video and my son Ryan, who is six, is sitting there watching it with me.

I have no idea if he is getting any of this. I am having enough trouble of my own so I just assume that maybe he just wants to spend a little time with the Old Man. I traveled too much at the time and was away from home far too often.

I do recall very clearly that the spokesperson on the video refers to the investment as a "wind farm" several times in this short tape. I am familiar with the term and at the time thought nothing of it.

Well, a short time after this Ryan is in school and his teacher asks each of the students to stand and tell all of the other kids in the class something about what their Dad does in his work.

When its Ryan's turn he stands and says "my Dads a wind farmer"! I can only imagine the reaction that got from not only the other six year olds but also his teacher.

I find out about all of this sometime later at a school function where his teacher tells me the story. Priceless! They may be ugly as I am walking among them now but I do have a smile on my face because of them.

That's it for now. I am doing my best to catch up and will try again tomorrow. Until then Buen

Camino and good night.

Saturday, June 1, 2013
Continuing on to Castrojeriz...stage 15, Dinner at La Taberna.

As I press on through the wind farm I catch up with Michele. It's actually getting very warm. I would guess that the temperature is closer to 70 than it is to 60. If this continues tomorrow could be a shorts day. That would be some change from the second day's snow storm.

I just woke up. It's Sunday and I am now writing the end of stage 15 which means I will be nearly caught up. I did see the pictures Robin selected for the posting. Nice job Honey, really nice job.

The only significant structure we will pass by today is a short distance from our destination. We will pass under The Arco de San Anton for St. Anthony of Egypt the patron Saint of Animals. The structure is over a thousand years old.

We arrive in the village of Castrojeriz and begin the search for our two Hotels. It is about 3:30, we have once again made good time. Before we begin searching for our Hotel's we will stop in at what turns out to be a famous Camino location.

As you enter this nice little place you immediately pick up the smell of something good coming from the Kitchen. The first room you enter is small and has two long tables positioned perpendicular to the bar. Michele heads to the bar and orders three small draft beers. He begins to speak with the owner.

Michele's understanding of and his passion for food pays off once again. We take a seat and out comes a combination of garlic stuffed green olives, the best and thinnest ham to date and a plate of cheese which has a coating of olive oil. The owner brings with him a bottle of Milcampos Tempernio, which is the icing on the cake.

The owner is now holding court with us and he and Michele are raving about the dish and other combinations. The owner is so engaged in the conversation that he decides to just turn around take two steps to the front door and lock it! He just closed and its 3:45. He will open again but for now he does not want any more customers to distract him from this conversation. We now have a private room. As I am sitting right next to the door I can see all of the people trying to come in banging on the door, the owner just ignores them. It's good to be King.

He goes back to the kitchen and returns with other types of ham and he also brings a book. He begins to explain to Michele that the book which was written by a very famous German author mentions the restaurant we are sitting in. Both Rainer and Michele immediately recognize the authors name and they begin to discuss his writings. Now the owner is very happy.

Long story short. The writer decides to just drop everything one day and head to the Camino sometime around 2001. When he completes the Camino he writes about it and it becomes a huge success in Germany and is directly connected to the increase in the number of Germans who walk the Camino.

The author, Hape Hans Peter as best I understand the explanation refers to the restaurant La Taberna where we are seated, as the best restaurant on The Camino. He shows the page where the comment is made. Michele asks if we can return for dinner and the owner reserves a table for us at 8:30. I think it's going to be very good.

We check into our Hotels. Michele could not get a room where Rainer and I are staying. The two Hotels are next to each other and basically share the same cafe- bar-front desk. We will meet there at 8:15.

Once the gear is taken care of there is a small opportunity to try to catch up on the blog, read a few emails and just relax after a shower.

I feel fine, no significant health issues so far as I am approaching the half way point! It's time to return to dinner. Michele is talking to a new pilgrim I have not met before. His name is Rainer and he is from Germany. He started his Camino in Burgos which means he just finished his second day. He does not know if he will continue it's been very tough. He has no idea what hard is!

He turns to me and says that Michele told him that I am 65 and that I have walked 15 days starting in St. Jean. He asks me if that is true? I tell him yes and he says he does not know how I could do it because he is only 59 and is thinking about quitting. I just stay quite. What I wanted to say was stay away from the buffet table and you might make it. I nick name him Burgos Ray. Time will tell.

The three of us leave for dinner and we are not disappointed. The restaurant has three people working there: the owner, his wife and his son. They are all equally passionate about their restaurant and its food and wine.

We sit and the son is talking with Michele about the menu. All I understand is that we must have the garlic soup. We all do and it's very good. The wine is selected by Rainer, it's a reserve Rioja. I have the blue fish and a salad and it's all as good as I had thought it would be.

It's late, I am tired. Back to the Hotel Stage16 tomorrow will be to Fromista, a walk of 16.1 miles with two significant hills. The first and most difficult hill comes quickly and has an elevation change of about 600 feet.

Burgos Ray will be facing his first real test tomorrow but he's lucky because at least it's not going to snow.

Until tomorrow, good night.

Saturday, June 1, 2013
To Fromista stage 16...its official, Margaret has gone home, her Camino has ended.

Margaret's Camino has ended. But we push on. Our next objective is stage 16 Fromista. There will be an early test on this 16 mile stage. Sixteen miles is a long segment.

Michele and I leave just ahead of Rainer. It is a nice day, a bit chilly but the hill we climb just one mile into stage 16 will provide lots of opportunity to get warm quickly. We are moving at a good pace when I look ahead and see what is starting to look like a traffic jam.

It's the hill. Wow. Even from where we are I can see that is a challenge. There are a number of pilgrims scattered on the trail to the top. Lots of pilgrims stopping to catch their breath and drink whatever it is they are carrying. This will not be a single shot march to the top.

We take the first half of the 600 feet rise in good time passing many others. That's the way it's supposed to be. Just go at your own pace and don't worry about how long it takes to get to the top, just get to the top.

I stopped well before we started up to take a picture. It's an attempt to let you see what lies ahead. I don't know if it will show up but if I'm not too far away it should work. I also stop half way up and then again at the top and take pictures looking back. The village of Castrojeriz should be visible and may provide some perspective. I will send these to Robin.

At the top there are a number of pilgrims resting and also celebrating the climb. Some are waiting for others. Burgos Ray will surely be pushed today. I just changed his name to Ray because it's just easier to remember and spell. Burgos Ray, it has a nice ring to it.

Just over the top of the hill there is a small monument with a simple plate which tells the story of a young man, age 42, who reached the top of the hill and died at this point. Sad, but it happens. I am glad that I was not aware of this before we left today.

From this point on there is very little to see that is more interesting than anything I have seen thus far. It will be just a long walk in the sun. It's a nice day, sunny and mild. It will not be long before I am down two layers and sweating. My feet are fine; my minor toe issue has been taken care of. It's sore but it won't get in the way.

There is almost zero shade. Water is not readily available but I have what I need. Just keep going. Michele and I are making good time when we catch up with Anna. We are now all walking together and as I stop to take pictures or drink some water Anna and Michele are moving very well ahead of me. Soon the gap between us is probably a half mile.

This trail is visible for miles ahead. The wind is up a little but it's not a problem. The only "attraction" today (at least for me) is the Canal De Castilla, built in the 18th century for transporting people and goods; it is now used only for irrigation.

I am about nine miles into the walk and I can see a small group of buildings about a mile ahead. I get closer and Anna is standing outside this small Albergue waving at me to come inside. Michele and Anna have stopped, and Anna is having some problem with her right foot or heal. Michele has something like a sports cream which heats up once you apply it. They are discussing in Spanish if it will help with Anna's problem. She decides not to use it.

After a Coke Zero we are heading back out again, all three of us. It's not long before Michele and I pull away as Anna takes a slower pace.

We reach Fromista in very good time. Michele is staying at a different Hotel which we come to first. My Hotel is just a couple hundred yards past his. We stop and have a short beer as a reward for today's effort. I am for the first time in two days hungry.

Rainer and I are staying at the same Hotel and we agree to meet back at this location at 8:00 before dinner. Reservations at 8:30 at what turns out to be the best restaurant we have been to so far.

Rainer knows what he's doing when it comes to a lot of things on The Camino. Food and wine are at the top of his list. I remind myself just how blessed I am to have met these two guys.

We meet back at the cafe and all of the "children" have arrived and gathered there. Rainer and I call them the children because they are for the most part very young. Today there are several new faces. I take a seat and introduce myself to a young guy next to me. His name is Fernando. He lives in Spain and this is his first Camino. I would guess that he is 25.

Grab a glass of wine. Really, go and get one.

He asks me "why are you walking the Camino"? His English is pretty good, much better than my nonexistent Spanish. My response is simple. "Mine is a walk of gratitude". I can see he is confused. I attempt to tell him more but what I want to tell him he will not understand. But I will share it with you.

When Ryan was just three years old he got sick like all three year olds do. You know a cold, an ear infection, maybe even the flu.

He was sick for about a week and his mother took him to the Pediatrician twice in just a couple of days because he was not getting any better. First diagnosis: the flu. I was working and fortunately not far away as would normally be the case.

I get a call and his mother has made what will turn out to be a critical decision to take him to the emergency room. That decision will save his life. I am on my way.

At the Bridgeport Hospital we are being looked after by a very young Doctor. Everyone in the emergency room is coming by to say hello and to of course tell us just how cute Ryan is. Some time passes by and I go to the front desk and I can't help but notice that all of the people who were so nice are suddenly not able or are trying to avoid making eye contact with me. I can sense that something is wrong, terribly wrong. I will never forgive the Pediatrician for what happened next. Never.

He is on the phone and wants to speak to both me and Ryan's mother at the same time. There are two phones there at the emergency room desk. We are on the phone when the Pediatrician says "Ryan has Leukemia". I cannot put into words what I felt at that moment.

We are taken to a private room and the young Doctor who we had met a couple of hours ago walks in and hands me a brochure about the treatment of Leukemia! I can't think straight but I do recall that I asked him to leave us alone immediately. He apparently skipped the class on bedside manners or on how to deal with real people who have just been given the most terrifying news they had ever heard.

Ryan's Mother and I discuss this news and the decision is easy. We must get Ryan to Yale New Haven Hospital now where he can get the best Pediatric care. I grab Ryan and as I walk out I tell the young Doctor to call Yale and tell them we are on our way. He tells me that I can't just take Ryan and leave. I tell him to call Yale in a way that could not be any clearer. Nothing is going to keep us from leaving.

It's only about 30 miles to Yale. We arrive and they have been told we were on our way. They are ready for us. Ryan and his mother are taken into another room where the Doctors on duty immediately begin to figure out what to do. I am left to first complete the admission paperwork. It's about 2:00 am.

I will never forget watching the clerk begin typing on an old electric typewriter Ryan's name and then going on to the next line and typing in each letter on the card...LEUKEMIA.

Ryan is admitted to the children's cancer ward. The nightmare just keeps getting worse. We are now in a small but private dark room. Ryan is in a crib, lifeless and his color tells the entire story. He looks very bad. I am scared to death.

I need to walk and think. He is sleeping. I get on the elevator and when the door closes I hit the stop button and get on my knees and ask God to save my son. I have never told anyone this before.

I return to the room. There is no change in Ryan, he is still sleeping. The door opens slightly and two young Doctors come in and sit on the floor across from me, a young woman and a young man. The young man begins to ask me questions about Ryan and as politely as I can I ask them to come back later. I have answered these same questions a number of times in the last three hours.

At that moment I hear the young woman whisper to her partner "I don't think its Leukemia." I am now awake to say the least. I turn to both of the young Doctors sitting on the floor in the dark and I said «I heard that». At that moment I have the first sense of hope. I press them to tell me about what I just heard her say. They are both silent. I don›t think I was supposed to hear that. I press harder.

The two young Doctors whisper among themselves and they are clearly concerned that they have allowed me to hear something that will cause them problems. They have spoken out or order or turn. I'm not sure what it's called and I don't care. I want a response.

In what seems like an eternity the young man does respond. "We think it's something else." This is my first ray of hope. He says "we think that its Heremic Uremic Syndrome." (Please forgive the spelling it's really not important.) I am thrilled because they think it's not Leukemia. I understand Leukemia. I know nothing about what they have just told me but I hope that it's better.

I will shorten the details but at 7:00 that morning the entire staff of Doctors in the unit are with us telling us to not get ahead of ourselves. I understand now why the two young Doctors on the floor at 4:00 am were nervous when I heard what they said.

They need to have a sample of Ryan's bone marrow and that's a surgical procedure which we instantly approve. The test comes back; the young Doctors have it right! Treatment is immediate including potassium and blood. We now wait.

In less than twenty four hours Ryan is Ryan again! It is a miracle. Ryan's disease is the first case of its kind at Yale and one of only a handful diagnosed in the US. I will never know what would have happened if first his mother had not had the good sense to get Ryan to a hospital and we did not just up and leave and get him to Yale.

I thank the two young Doctors for having been willing to step out of being comfortable for their own benefit and getting it right. But most of all I thank Him for listening to me when I was in that elevator.

I am now glad that the young Spaniard who asked me why I was walking The Camino did not speak perfect English. It has given me an opportunity to tell a story which I have kept to myself for more than thirty years.

I am drained. I will complete this post about stage 16 tomorrow. I know you will understand. Good night Ryan, I hope you are well. Love Dad.

Sunday, June 2, 2013
Stage 17, a short walk to Carrion De Los Condes...I meet The Candy Man of The Camino.

I am now more than half way to Santiago. Today the distance is not only a short 12 miles, it is also flat. No challenges today.

Today's blog will also be much shorter than my previous posts. Yes, it's your lucky day. No wine needed.

Michele comes to meet Rainer and me at our Hotel. It is 9:00. Rainer and I have had breakfast and I am packed and ready to go when Michele arrives. Rainer will leave after us and as is now the norm we will meet for dinner.

We are moving very quickly. There will be nothing once we pass the last cafe about two miles from our starting point. We will stop there. Michele has not had breakfast and wants something to eat with his cafe. I am just not hungry in spite of today's "breakfast" being next to nothing.

I order a cafe-con leche. I really can't get use to the beard and the con leche combination but I am trying. Michele orders a bocadillo and we take a seat outside. It's cold today and the wind is blowing pretty hard. It will really get going once we get into the open. There will be nothing to slow it down and it will be the only challenge.

Almost on cue from around the corner Fernando and Nelly arrive. Michele as always, in his booming voice shouts out "Brazil". This has now become the standard greeting for the Brazilian couple.

Nelly is bundled up with a wool hat, gloves, a turtle neck sweater and her rain jacket. She looks like she is looking for a Double Blue Run in Aspen! I ask her if she is going skiing and she laughs and interprets for Fernando who just laughs and says "Jim, Jim, Jim". He thinks I'm funny.

We finish our visit and wish them Buen Camino and head back to The Camino. From that point on this piece of The Camino is a combination of trail and roads. The roads are not busy so it's just making the walk that much faster. The wind is howling and it's getting colder because of it.

We are on a pace to get to De Los Condes in less than four hours. At about the half way point you have two routes to choose from. The trail route and the road route for the second half. The road route will be faster but it's a busy road even on a Sunday. We select the trail; we don't need to be any faster. Camino rules. If one of us wanted to take the road route no problem we would just split up and meet later. I wonder if the Weather Girl has figured this out yet.

Here is only one thing that makes today's walk special. There's always something. The trail is narrow and we are walking single file. I see a man up ahead, an older man. He is looking at us as we approach. He is holding a bag of something.

He says to me in a very bold voice "Buen Camino", reaches into his bag and hands me two wrapped pieces of candy. He then offers to shake my hand and is speaking to me in Spanish. I don't know what he is saying. He repeats the candy process with Michele. We visit.

The Candy Man, a name I have now given him, tells Michele that he has spent every day for the past 12 years driving to points along the Camino close to his home to keep in good repair the Camino signs which help direct the pilgrims. He points to the sign behind us where he has just cut the grass with a hand tool. I have a picture.

We thank him several times and he sends us on our way. This was the highlight of the day. We arrive shortly thereafter to De Los Condes. We stop for a short beer. Then we went on to our different Hotels.

Dinner is at 7:00 with Rainer and a couple of the "children". It's okay but not memorable. This was an early night. It will be needed because tomorrow stage 18 will be the longest walk of the entire journey. Tomorrow I will walk for the 18th consecutive day, a walk of 21 miles.

That's it for now. I told you it would be your lucky day.

Tuesday, June 4, 2013
A long walk today...17 miles. Bad news from Brazil.

In my last post I made an error and said that today would be 21 miles. That was incorrect. It will be long but not 21 miles, just 17. Today will be different in a number of ways. I will also include a short summary at the end of this post regarding the nightmare of those two days years ago at the Hospital. I could not finish and include the ending; it was too difficult to go any further. It is a good ending and I want to close with what took place after Ryan's recovery.

First today is Monday June the 3rd. I am awake early and have just started to pack when the first issue of the day is in front of me. Most of last night's laundry is not dry. Zip locks to the rescue. I will just deal with the problem at the end of today's journey.

I have plenty of Veep left. I think I should contact the Veep detergent company and ask about a US distribution deal. Just think. "Veep, the Camino Pilgrims Friend". It still needs work but I am close to finishing my work on the final logo. I can't share that with you, top secret.

I head to breakfast. It's 9:15. I get my coffee and order a ham and cheese sandwich. Not a bocadillo. It's okay because that's all there is. I am nearly finished and Rainer joins me. Michele is staying at a different Hotel and has started early today on The Camino. He is walking with a few people from his Hotel. They all need to get to the same Albergue that I am staying in but not later than 4:00 pm or their rooms could be given away. I am prepaid so I can leave when I choose to. Thank You Sharel.

Rainer is skipping today's segment. It's long and he's done it twice before. He has told me several times it's about his least favorite part of the Camino. I get it. In my eyes he can't do anything wrong. It's another blessing that I am walking the Camino with my own tour guide. I would carry his backpack if he asked me to. I will soon share with you another situation where one person carries another pilgrim's backpack for more than 7 miles.

Remember Janet from Indiana? It's a repeat performance by Michele but it's not Janet from Indiana.

Back to breakfast. As I am ordering my sandwich Fernando and Nelly are getting ready to leave. Fernando stops by the table to say Buenos Dias. I ask him how is foot is? We don't speak a word of each other's language but we seem to understand each other pretty well.

Nelly was busy paying for their breakfast and joins Fernando and immediately begins interpreting. As for Fernando's foot Nelly explains that ten years ago Fernando hurt his foot while working in the building trade. That is a tough business. I can only imagine how many other injuries he has had, its tough work.

I can say that because I worked as a laborer for two summers for a great man named Harry. I was a 17 year old junior in high school and my partner in completely botching up every task we were given was Mike, an 18 year old senior.

When I have told people about those two years I will laugh so hard while I do it that I will come close to breaking a rib. All you need to do is ask my brother Rick and his wife Jill to tell you what's it like to hear what Mike and I did.

Ever lose a dump truck? Poor cement on a wedding cake the day of the wedding? Have you ever cut down the wrong fifty trees? I could go on but this is not the time or place. Robin says I should write a book. I don't think so.

My point is I understand how Fernando could be injured in his line of work.

Back to the Camino stage 18. According to a number of guide books I have now taken more than 530,000 steps and have about 470,000 ahead of me. I am packed and ready to get started. I will be walking alone today and that›s just fine.

I leave the Hotel at about 9:30. I need to get some hand cream because my hands are fried and the passengers in my Limos would also like some attention. There is a drug store on the way. I saw it last night. I hope it's open before 10:00.

It is open. I use some gestures with my hands and she understands. She then places three tubes of hand cream on the counter; I guess this is where I decide between doors one, two or three. I pick number two. She smiles which I think means she agrees with my choice. The hand cream cost is 8.90 Euro about $11.25 US.

That's more than all but two of the bottles of red wine I had in the villages.

My next stop is the Camino shop. I am hoping that they will sell cheap sunglasses. The Camino shop in Pamplona did and I have not been able to find a replacement for the missing second pair. I really need them. Yesterday with the wind blowing and the sun light bouncing off the white trail my eyes are constantly dry or tearing. Today's walk conditions and length will be very tough on my eyes if I can't find glasses.

I am in luck! I see a rack of sunglasses in the rear. Well, it's a rack but there are only four choices. One pair is immediately eliminated because I know without even trying that they won't fit my Mellon. Another pair is yellow, I don't think so. Two remain to choose from. Anybody ever heard of Coco Channel? There they are. No, I can't do it. I want to so I can bring them home for Pat to wear when he walks the Camino in August but I select the only other pair. My eyes are saved!

Last stop before I get to the Camino. I need water and something to eat along the way. The guide book says there is not much available and water is in short supply so I must bring enough with me. That will mean a little extra weight. Two liters of water weighs about four pounds.

I go to the local market and just can't find anything to bring to eat along the way. I do get my water and I do pick up a couple of things for lunch.

Lunch today will be a combination of an orange, dark Swiss chocolate and a small bag of almonds. Yes, the Camino lunch. Perhaps when I return I can get Jaxier to put it on the menu in the Men's Grill. The Camino lunch available at Dove, just in case its cart path only and you have to actually walk to your ball.

With my new sunglasses, water and lunch I start my 17 mile hike.

The weather is good. It's cool and the wind is up but nothing like yesterday. The first two miles of the walk today is on or alongside paved roads. There isn't much traffic but whenever there is you pay attention. These people drive fast and the roads are not very wide. I always walk on the side of the road with traffic approaching me. If I can see them coming toward me I have a better chance if I need to get out of the way than if the problem is coming at me from the rear. I don't care which side of the road the Camino arrow is painted on.

Once I get to the trail I am already sweating and I need to get rid of my jacket. It's still cool but I have become use to this combination. I will also for the first time tie my poles to my backpack. They won't be needed today and it will be easier to walk without them.

The guide book was correct. It's flat, there is not much to see accept miles and miles of wheat and corn. In front the view is exactly the same for the next 15 miles. A light colored trail that is straight and just looks endless.

I am moving at a pace that has me passing many pilgrims. I catch up and pass Fernando and Nelly. They left at least an hour before me. Not long after I pass them I catch up with Michele, Emily, Anna, Emma and Bono. I will explain Bono later. I don't like him.

As I get closer I can see that something is wrong. Michele is carrying two backpacks. His own on his back and a second strapped to his chest. The second one belongs to Anna. Her left leg is badly swollen and she is using her poles like canes. From this location we are at least 7 miles from the only tiny village before the final stop.

I ask him if he wants to spread the weight of Anna's bag among all of us to make it a little better. He says no. Her bag is smaller and he feels balanced. Michele and I move on. There is no point in lagging back trying to walk at the pace needed for Anna. That would be worse.

We march on. We are making very good time actually passing quite a few pilgrims, some we know. Michele tells me that Anna's leg is not the only issue; in fact it's the smaller issue she is dealing with. Anna's sister contacted her late last night to tell her that her Father died suddenly.

I thought when I saw her crying back on the trail it was the leg problem. I now understand what the real problem is. I assume she will fly back to Brazil as soon as possible but Michele tells me that Anna's sister has told her to complete the Camino. It's what her Father would want her to do.

We both agree on one thing. Anna must take a donkey service to the next hotel or in this case the Albergue where we are all staying. It's the only place to stay and from the village we are now quickly approaching its six miles. Hopefully there will be some way to find her a ride. She can't walk much longer.

Michele and I arrive at the next, only and last village before the final destination. As we make a turn following the Camino markers there it is, a taxi. I never would have guessed that there would be any taxi service here. Michele finds the driver in the cafe and books the car before anyone else can. The cost to take Anna to the Albergur is 15 Euro. This is cheap to say the least.

The group arrives but Anna is still lagging behind. She is struggling. Once she does arrive the cafe guy gives her a bag of ice for her leg and the driver is ready when she is. We sit for about thirty minutes and have what is a well-deserved bocadillo. Once Anna and her backpack are loaded we all leave and soon thereafter we are in multiple groups. Pace, that's all that matters.

I am first to arrive and the Albergue is fairly new and clean. I get my room and go back to meet Rainer for a beer. Rainer took the donkey service and arrived a couple of hours ago. As we are having our beer he asks me if I will use the laundry service. Laundry service? He explains.

At this Albergue you can have all of your laundry washed for 4 Euro. Sign me up! I am given a rubber bucket and told to just bring it back to the desk and they will handle it. I follow her instructions and bring back basically everything I have and just throw on a pair of shorts and a tee shirt. It's really warmed up and the sun is out. It's a really nice day.

About an hour later as we are now all gathered in the cafe the woman I gave my laundry to walks up to our table and drops the rubber bucket next to me. It's my laundry. It's been washed but it's all wet. At that moment I find out that now I need to take the wet clothes and go out back and hang them all on the clothesline. Everybody says they want a picture of me hanging my laundry! They all think it will be very funny, especially Fernando and Nelly.

I do go outside get the needed clothes pins and get started. Everyone can't wait and now the picture session begins. Yes I have a picture which will be sent to Robin.

Ok, now that that's been taken care of its time for dinner. I did think for just a second that perhaps I should find out where the laundry room is to see if they are using Veep. It would give me some valuable competitive info!

Dinner is not very good. It's not supposed to be, it's a pilgrim meal but once again the salad is very good, very fresh. I don't eat much of the main course pasta because it's just not good. No problem, I'm not very hungry.

Rainer, Michele and I retire to the cafe- bar-reception desk. The owner, a very nice lady begins a conversation with Rainer as he checks out the small selection of wine on the counter. They chat and she leaves and returns with three bottles that are not on display. They are all Crienza quality. We each order a glass of the Rioja, its good and she is pleased that we approve. Rainer asks if she has any Reserva or Alta Rioja. She goes into the back room again and returns with a Casis 2006 Gran Reserva which was a Gold Medal winner in 2012. She is very proud of the wine and goes into great detail about how famous the wine is. Rainer asks her how much? She says it's not for sale. It's the only bottle she has. She turns to help other customers and while she is gone we huddle about the wine.

When she returns we make her a Godfather like offer. You know "an offer she can't refuse". She caves. It was worth every penny. I am sitting here tasting this really terrific wine waiting to go back outside to take my clothes off the clothesline. It's the Camino, it happens.

It's been a long day and tomorrow will be another 17 miles, stage 19. But first as promised the final piece of the Ryan Hospital nightmare. It's good.

As I wrote in my last post Ryan was given what was needed to save him. He was fully recovered in less than forty eight hours. We are taking him home and one of the young Doctors tells me another good piece of news. The research they have shown that in all of the cases, about two thousand in the US, there has never been relapse, never.

The Doctors ask if we would be willing to bring Ryan back once a month so they can monitor his blood and generally his development for the next two years. Yale has never had another "Ryan" and getting to study him will be of great value in helping them and others better understand this disease. There was never any hesitation.

For nearly the next two years we take Ryan to Yale. I can only hope that the nightmare of that night has helped save just one other 3 year old.

That's it for now, I'm tired. I will leave Bono for tomorrow. Good night.

Tuesday, June 4, 2013
Stage 19...I just walked 17 miles in less than 5 and a half hours...That's great, but I missed a turn, I'm in the wrong town!

Not a problem. I will provide details soon. But first a brief update on the group. Most are doing just fine but some are having increasing issues.

I have not seen Mee-sue in two days. That does not mean much. She could be ahead or just slowed down a little. Burgos Ray was last seen yesterday when he decided to stop at an Albergue about six miles short of where everyone else finished stage 18. That means he is now facing a continuous adjustment but that will be difficult because stage 19 and 20 are very long and there are not many options. I doubt I will see him again unless he takes the donkey service. Anna is hurting but very determined. I believe she will just press on.

The rest of the crew is fine but tired. I saw lots of ice bags last night at the Albergue. Ice around here is scarce but you can find it. Sports creams are at a premium.

Now for Bono. It was about five or six days ago when he first showed up. He just latched onto the group. Why have I given him the name Bono? Well the guy just never takes off his sunglasses, day or night. Maybe if I did that I might have the first or second pair I lost. Not the point.

I think he was attracted to the group because of the number of young woman in the group. He is from Montenegro. I get a bad vibe from this guy. I would guess he is about 45 years old. I just don't like the way he circles the girls. I also know that a couple of them are not entirely comfortable around him. I sat next to him twice, not by choice. I know that when he is near me he is careful and I am certain he knows I have him pegged right.

Time will tell and I hope my vibe is off. I don't think so. I would hate to see Bono have to get a new pair of sunglasses. I will keep you posted.

Today I am walking 17 miles, stage 19. Today also is two weeks from the day I will walk into the Cathedral of Santiago. This has taken just two weeks or about 200 miles. My destination today is (was) Calzadilla de Los Hermanillos but I will end up in Bercianos Del Real Camino. How you ask did this happen?

Rainer, Michele and I have coffee and decide that we will have something to eat at the first village. Just like yesterday it will be long, flat and straight. It will also be for the first time hot, probably around 80 degrees. We will have breakfast in Mortatinos. Good decision. Scrambled egg and melted cheese bocadillo. The bread is fresh, and it's put back in the oven for just seconds and its perfect. The coffee is also better than what we had before we left the Albergue.

Aside from the wrong turn I think this bocadillo will be the highlight of the day. Today I have taken very few pictures. It's just a duplicate of yesterday, but it is hot and there is no shade. Once we get past our first break location there will be very little until we get to Newark, sorry I meant Sahagun a city of 170,000. Completely lacking in anything that's attractive I can only assume that all 170,000 must be prisoners. Why on earth would you stay here unless forced to? It's a dump. Sorry, that's probably not going to put me on the Sahagun tourist of the year list.

So here›s the wrong turn. I am walking through the city. I am ahead of the entire group. My pace today is faster. Can›t explain it but when it›s working and there›s no physical reason to slow down you just go. The downside is you are not following anyone you know who is going to the same place you are.

In every large city I have walked through, except Pamplona, the Camino markers have been at best poorly maintained. The Camino today has two routes. One is the Roman path and one is the Camino Frances. In the middle of Sahagun the two Camino's split. One easterly route the other to the west. Tomorrow they will join again but not again today. So I am not lost and I am not off the Camino. I am just not going to be able to get to the room I have booked.

So here I am nearly six hours of walking at a very good pace and I can see the town up ahead. It's the only town or village I have seen since Sahagun about six miles ago. Great, I will get to the town at about 3:15 in plenty of time to take care of my gear, take a shower, rest my Limo passengers and then wait until everyone arrives.

I enter the town and immediately begin looking for my Casa. It's the Casa el Cura. I see signs for the municipal Albergue but nothing for my Casa. I walk past the Hotel Rivero but still no Casa del Cura. I have the hotel name printed in my notes on my iPhone so I can just ask by showing the address and ask "Donde es Casa del Cura"? I try this twice but no response.

I get to what is clearly the end of town and I double back. There is a bar-cafe at the entrance to the town. I will ask there. I show the young woman behind the counter my iPhone, after I order a small beer, and she says in perfect English, "you missed the turn". I take out my guide book and I open it and she points to the turn back in Sahagun and then she points to where the Casa is and then to where we are located. This is not good. Yes, the Camino will join together before my next destination but where will I find a room now for tonight?

I am already thinking that I may have to sleep in one of the bunk bed Albergue's! They may also be full. I pick up my gear and make my way back to that Hotel I saw, the Rivero. I walk in and the young woman behind the counter starts asking me questions in Spanish at light speed. She figures out quickly that I have a problem when I respond to the only thing she has said that I think I understand "reservation?" No.

She yells something to someone and an older woman comes to the counter. She speaks a little English but enough for her to know that I am asking for a single room. She grabs a key and starts toward the stairs. I follow her. She stops at number 5 and unlocks the door. I look in; there are two very small twin beds, a window and a sink. No shower. Before I can say anything she turns around and opens a door across the hall. It's a bathroom with a shower and she tells me that's it mine included for 25 Euro. I say Si and I now have a room and it has Wi-Fi.

I begin sending emails to a Robin and Sharel. Wrong turn—no big deal. Tomorrow a walk of about 16.5 miles to where the two Camino's join again. I am on my way to Mansilla de las Mulas, or at least that's where I am going to try and get to. It's all part of the journey. Good night.

Tuesday, June 4, 2013
Stage 20. Do sheep ever sleep?...my room overlooks the barnyard. I can't count the bah,bah,bahs.

Why is it that some people believe that if you can't sleep all you need to do is simply count sheep and you will soon be fast asleep? Trust me it's not true especially when the sheep don't sleep. As I write this I can hear the rooster just outside my window telling me to get started on stage 20. I give up. I will leave early today.

I slept with the window open all night because it was warm and I have no chance of sleeping in a warm room. Also working with the sheep are the two very large people in the next room. I now understand what it's like to hear snoring at the professional level.

I am packed and will soon leave after the morning fix of cafe-con-leche and a pound of carbs. Speaking of carbs I have had a couple of people ask me about how the Camino is affecting my weight. Well I am not sure but that's not all that significant. I think the carbs and the Rioja are a good offset. I do believe I have lost some weight but I have no idea how much. Remember the list of items not included in my room a couple of days ago? If I missed it add a scale.

A few months back if you had asked me why I was doing this I would be somewhat vague but I almost always said "lose some weight". That is now gone from my list. If it happens great, but if not that's fine.

I also received an email that actually made me laugh. A friend at the Club suggested that after I complete the Camino I should think about a three day hike in the Grand Canyon! Sammy, I think you need to get out of the sun, it can be dangerous. I'm not sure about a lot of things but I am sure that I will not be hiking the Grand Canyon!

When I get back and have rested a bit I will return to seeing Edwin three days a week. I will probably walk to and from those sessions which is about eight miles round trip. I will be wearing my Nike Town Cars; my Limos will be retired and mounted in my office. I'm not kidding—I will have my Limos in a glass case.

Back to stage 20. This is a walk of 17 miles to my room at the Hostal San Martin. I have read the map and there is only one turn and it takes place in Mansilla de las Mullas. The trail today will be long, flat and windless. It will also be hot, about 90 degrees. That will require lots of water because the first and only stop will not be until the tenth mile.

If I take four liters of water that will add four pounds to my backpack. Add some food and you start to have a weight issue. This will be the third day in a row where extra water is needed and it will have an impact. I can already feel the difference in my shoulders and hips.

I order half a bocadillo with ham, cheese and tomato to go. It's big, about a half loaf of bread. Good bread, carbs all carbs. I also bring an orange in spite of the added weight. The oranges here are not only good they are large.

I am on the Camino and I am passing a number of pilgrims I have not seen before. There are many who begin at the half way point or later. In order to receive a Compostela in Santiago you must start at or before Sarria which is 133.9 km or about 84 miles. If the first stamp in your Camino Passport is in Sarria you must have a minimum of two stamps per day from there to Santiago. Forget to have two stamps, no Compostela.

The trail is narrow and getting around two pilgrims walking side by side can only be accomplished by making sure they hear you. Just a Buen Camino as you approach them and you will be given a clear path.

I am now approaching a guy I have never seen before. He is wearing ear plugs and is singing and having a good time. As I pass him I just wave and he does the same, he obviously can't hear me. I will soon find out more about "The Singer". That's the name I have given him.

At about the seven mile mark I can see one person sitting on a Camino marker. He looks familiar. It's Fernando and Nelly. They also missed the turn! It's not just me. I yell out to him "Brazil" and he responds with a nickname he gave me when I bought my new 7 Euro sunglasses, "James Bond"!

I stop and take off my backpack. It's been a tough walk and it's getting harder because of the heat. Nelly is limping. She shows me her left leg. It's swollen and there is a rash above her ankle. She goes on to explain that she wore two pairs of socks yesterday and the heat became a problem. They will visit a Doctor when they get to Mansilla.

The conversation switches to how we both missed the turn. Fernando is of course laughing as he tries to explain to me in Portuguese, with Nelly interpreting what happened. Long story, they saw the same marker I did. I think they are relieved that they were not the only ones to make the mistake. I decide that it's a good time for my Orange. While we are sitting there "the singer" catches up with us. Nelly tells me that they met the "Singer" at their Hostal last night, he is Brazilian. They chat for a minute and he puts his ear plugs in and waves goodbye and leaves.

Nelly then tells me that he started in St Jean six days after we did and that he is averaging about 24 miles a day and will complete the Camino in just 24 days. He obviously is a better walker than he is a singer.

We pack up and get back to the job at hand. It's now officially hot. I don't know what the temperature is I just know it's hot. I am also consuming the water at a pretty good clip. There is one and only one tiny place about two miles ahead. I will stop for water.

The balance of the 17 miles is just the same. Dead straight, flat without wind, no shade and hot. I yearn for a rain shower. As I leave the little water station I catch up with a young girl who I have seen with the other children. She is very bright and very confident. She has traveled a great deal for someone as young as she is. I remember her because of her first and middle name. Braydyn Ryan. My grandson's name is Brayden, a slightly different spelling and my son's name is as you know, Ryan. I forgot to mention it a couple of days ago. I have missed a bunch of things, no big deal.

I am in the Hostal and I cannot wait to get in the shower. Room seven. I take care of my gear and then a shower. My Limo passengers are really tired and for the first time sore. It was just a matter of time. Speaking of time I covered the 17 miles in less than six hours and I did not make a single wrong turn.

This will not make any sense but after I take a shower I take a walk back into town. Taking a walk after 17 very tough miles makes no sense but I need a couple of things and the market is back in town about a half mile away.

I bump into a couple of the children and they all agree that today was very difficult. I agree and I am on my way back to the Hostal. I have not seen any of others, just Fernando and Nelly. Rainer sent me an email that he has gone on to Leon. We will meet there tomorrow for dinner.

That's stage 21 to Leon. The walk will cover a distance of only 12 miles. It's like a day off! Good night.

Thursday, June 6, 2013
The Nordic guy in the short-shorts can't get past the old man...He's not happy.

Stage 21 to Leon, a city with a population of about 130,000. My walk today will be just 12 miles. I have packed and head down to breakfast. In this little Hostal, breakfast just does not happen. The choices are a packaged muffin or a packaged muffin. I do have orange juice and coffee but pass on today's fine selection of previously prepared, wrapped in plastic carb delivery systems. I will find something on the Camino.

I will leave today earlier than most other days. Today I step foot on the Camino at 8:20 more than an hour ahead of most departures. I would like to get to Leon and have some time to see the center of the city as well as The Cathedral.

As I start out the weather is very nice. Probably around 65 with a little cloud cover and a hint of a breeze. The Camino today will about half trail and half a combination of paved track alongside the road and paved walkways as I enter the city. It's a good day for walking. I have my water and I will find something to eat. The first cafe will be about 2 miles from the start.

There are only a few pilgrims on the Camino and my pace is already quick. The trails provide plenty of shade and today's walk will also be flat. As I am about a half mile into my day I can hear the loud crunching of someone's feet directly behind me. I will not turn to look but from the sound it must be a large person. I assume it's a man.

He must be twenty feet behind me but he is not getting any closer or trying to go by me. I have a thing about having someone this close behind me. I would prefer that they go by.

My pace is very quick and I can feel it in a positive way. No aches or pains I am just in a groove and I don't want to slow down and lose that. Speeding up would be the wrong thing to do and stopping to let him pass just disrupts my pace. I will just keep doing what I'm doing.

Suddenly the sound of his feet pounding the trail behind me is gone. I don't look back, he's taking a break. Good, now I can get back to just focusing on all of the thoughts that are bouncing around in my head. You have now been warned.

As I approach the cafe there are plastic chairs outside in the shade and I decide that I will get something to eat and sit there. As I am taking off my backpack I finally see him. He is as I suspected a large person, six foot five I would guess. He is bald and in his late 30's or early 40's. He is fit and he is wearing a black tank top, black knee brace on each knee and the shortest shorts I have ever seen on a man. These shorts would not get past Joe or Paul on the first tee.

As he passes me he is looking directly at me with a serious look of anger. I say Buen Camino and he just keeps going. I think he's mad because he could not get past the old man. Get over it! I hope he has a nice day. I doubt I will see him again. I hope I do though because I can't wait to see what other outfits he will be wearing on the Camino.

I continue. All is good I go into this small cafe in who knows where. I just want something to eat. I go inside and order a coffee. As the young woman hands me my cafe-con-leche I ask her for a bocadillo from the menu that's on the counter. She then explains in sign language that I now understand, that as the only person watching the store she cannot go in the back and make me a bocadillo. I get it. I will just drink my coffee and leave. No, wait. I see a free Wi-Fi sign on the wall. I will stay and I will buy one of those dreadful muffins which are wrapped in plastic. If I am going to use their free Wi-Fi the least I can do is buy something and be a customer.

I go on line, check email and send a couple of brief messages. It's the middle of the night in Capistrano. I send a message to Rainer that I will see him in Leon around 4:00 that afternoon.

The balance of the walk today is uneventful. I enter Leon and as is always the case entering the larger cities, finding your way is far more difficult. I am fast today.

As I enter the outskirts of the city I am focused on the route. I have made great time but I now need to pay attention to the map to get me to my hotel. I am fairly certain that I am on the correct path but I just need to verify it. There is a Farmacia on the corner just at the point where I will need to make a critical decision about direction. I will go in and ask for directions.

As soon as I walk in with my poles and backpack she knows I am on the Camino. She is the lady in the white coat. She takes one look at me and in perfect English she says "can I help you". I want help but I will first buy something. I ask if she has a cream for my sore feet (the passengers) and she quickly grabs a box off the shelf and says "this will help".

I follow her to the counter and pay for the cream. I then show her the name of my Hotel and ask her for help in getting there. She leads me to the front door, steps outside and simply points and says " three lights make a right, next light turn right again you will see it". I like these people.

I arrive at my hotel in really great time. It's only 2:00 and that means a quick shower and out to take care of something I need to do. It's a very nice hotel, very clean, modern, big, and comfortable. I check in.

When I get to my room the first thing I want to do is to unpack, plug in my iPad mini, check emails and shower. I need the password. Why can't they just give it to me when I check in?

I call the front desk. Yes, this hotel has a phone in the room and all of those other amenities. I am told that the password is too complex to give it to me over the phone and that it will be brought to me in writing shortly. This is a small delay in my plan. I can't get in the shower because I won't be able to answer the door so I wait.

Do you remember Lincoln's Gettysburg Address? "Four score and seven years ago, our Fathers ...." That small opening comment is shorter than my sign in ID and password for access to the hotel›s Wi-Fi, I kid you not.

After wasting the first hour of my visit to Leon trying to get on line I give up. After taking a shower I am soon back at the front desk. I ask about the Wi-Fi and for the first time since arriving in Spain I am facing someone who does not give a hoot about customer service.

I just take a deep breath and walk away. This desk person is very fortunate that she is dealing with AC Jim and not BC Jim or Travel Jim. Perhaps in the next blog I will explain who those Jim's are. I can just see the smiles on the faces of Robin, Maggie, Debbie, Alyce, Charles and others.

I just leave. I will not let this person poison my beliefs about all of the other people I have met. No, AC Jim will just let it go. I am disappointed because today is Amanda's 27th Birthday and I wanted to send a message. Here it is, Happy Birthday Amanda, I hope you have a great day! Love you, Dad.

That's it for now but one final comment before I hit publish. I am limping and have joined the ranks of the walking wounded. More later. Have a good day.

Friday, June 7, 2013
Stage 22 I will limp 13 miles to Mazarife...I have joined the ranks of the Walking Wounded.

I first began to feel it on my way to the Cathedral. My lower left leg is hurting. I am starting to limp. I guess it's the body's way of letting you know that you have gone a bit too fast today. I will just "walk it off". Wrong, very wrong.

I meet up with Rainer and Michele. We have been disconnected for a couple of days because I took that wrong turn. We have at least an hour before we will have dinner. I mentioned to Rainer that I need to buy socks. He knows where there is an outdoor shop, a small version of an REI. He is my own guide. He knows exactly how to get there. Unfortunately we are walking and my left leg is getting worse.

I buy what I need and we head to the Cathedral. It's really something to see. Rainer took a picture the night before I arrived and he emailed it to me. I will ask Robin to include it. The picture will allow me not to attempt to describe it.

Dinner is very good. We ate in a small place near the Cathedral. Rainer's first choice would cause us to wait longer. This place is fine. We walk back to the hotel. It seems like we are walking forever because my leg is getting worse with each step.

At breakfast I meet Michele and Rainer. I will be leaving after 10 because I must go to the department store for four items I will need in just a few days. I will tell you about them when that day arrives. It will be the most important part of my Camino.

Michele is staying in Leon. Our schedules will not match again until my final night in Santiago where we will have dinner and a Cuban cigar. Rainer will leave now and I will meet him later today in Mazarife at the Albergue, assuming I make it. Back up to my room to grab my gear, it's almost ten o'clock and the department store is directly across the street.

I return to the Lobby and waiting for me are Fernando and Nelly. They are staying in Leon for an extra day and Nelly's injury will cause them to add other stops to shorten their walks each day. This will be goodbye.

We take pictures, hugs all around and I am on my way to get what I need. I find them easily and back to the hotel for my gear. I start my 13 mile walk out of Leon. I am limping but if I just take it slow I will be fine.

I make more stops during this stage than any other prior stage. I will make one last stop in La Virgin Del Camino. It will be my last chance for food and water. Once I leave this cafe there will be a stretch of about 6 miles where there is nothing but the Camino.

I walk past one small cafe but I think I saw a sign that said Wi-Fi. I stop, go back and there is free Wi-Fi. I am the only customer. Two women are there, I am guessing mother and daughter. Mom is sitting at a table smoking and reading what looks like a tabloid newspaper. The daughter is working.

I order a Diet Coke and a bocadillo with ham, cheese and tomato. I pull out my iPad mini and plug it in. There is only one outlet and it's next to Mom's table. She says okay. I begin to check my email and I am standing next to Mom who is fascinated with my mini.

Robin sent me a video of Vivian a couple of days ago of El Gato playing with her Fun For Cats on Robin's iPad. It's an app that has a mouse running around the screen and Vivian loves it and it is a riot. I think why not show Mom how the mini works. I fire up the video and I show it to Mom. She goes nuts! She is just blown away and laughing wildly.

Her laughing brings the daughter out of the back to see what's going on. Mom is calling her to hurry and see this. I start it again. Same result times two. I think I made their day. The bocadillo was very good. I am my way again. One last comment about the cafe. The password for the Wi-Fi is 12345678. They should be running that fancy hotel.

There are two Camino's ahead just like the situation I was in two days ago. I will not make that mistake again. I have my map and guidebook. I must find the path that will turn left to take me to Mazarife. I find it and I am limping more noticeably.

I arrive at 5:15, not bad. I thought it would be at least another hour given my pace but I complete the walk in six hours and fifteen minutes. Now just find the Albergue. That's not very hard the town is about a five minute walk end to end.

I check in and the woman who handles the paperwork will now lead me to my private room with shared bath. Just a note. There are two types of Albergue's. All have giant sleeping rooms with bunk beds and tiny cots. Some also have private rooms like mine.

For the first time I will have to walk through the sleeping room with all of its occupants. I am about to have an anxiety attack! I cannot imagine staying in the non-private part of the Albergue. I am shown my room and the location of the shower down the hall. I drop my gear and head to the only cafe in town, Tio Pepi's. I know Rainer has arrived because I asked when I got here. I am correct. We have a beer. It's a nice little place and then Rainer tells me that they have rooms upstairs. Rooms? As in single rooms with baths? Yes. I ask "any available"? He asks the young girl behind the counter and she says Si. I am now looking at a picture of the room that is available and I take it. This will turn out to be a very good decision.

I am now headed back to the Albergue to gather my gear. I don't expect a refund and I would not ask. My leg is killing me and I just want to take a shower before Rainer and I head to the pilgrims dinner. I need to eat something. It's a pilgrim dinner. Salad excellent as always, soup not so good and the main course, it has yellow rice, vegetables and something else. I think it's the national dish, starts with a P, I can't spell it and I can't eat it. I am going to be hungry later.

There is one table of 14 pilgrims. I counted and there are three tables of four which Rainer and I fill in. The other two people sitting across from us are from Austria. The older of the two, probably in her seventies is wounded. She started well before us and she said that she will just take it slow. The other woman is younger; I'm guessing about 48 to 50. I guess that means 49. Give me some slack it's been a very difficult day.

I ask Monica where she started her Camino. She names a place in France and Rainer tells me that it's more than 1,000 miles! She then says, "Its two Camino's". I am a wimp. She goes on to say that her walk will be about 90 days.

We skip the dessert and head back to Tio Pepe's. It's about 7:30 and my leg is really becoming a problem. Loli to the rescue. It just keeps getting better! Good night.

Saturday, June 8, 2013
Price only matters in the absence of value...Loli proves me right.

I am blessed and my decision to give up my prepaid private room with shared bath at the Albergue proves that what I have been preaching for more than thirty years is correct. Price only matters in the absence of value.

We return to Tio Pepe's. Rainer and I are in the cafe-bar-reception desk and I drop my 7 Euro sunglasses and they break into two pieces. My third pair is now gone. I pick them up and put the two pieces on the bar. I order a small beer and head to my room to get a Ziploc bag, I need ice and I need it now. I am facing a twenty mile walk tomorrow which is looking more and more impossible with each step I take and I'm not wearing a 23 pound backpack.

I return, limping more than ever when the woman behind the counter says "no" when I ask for ice while holding out the zip lock. Then she disappears but soon returns with a frozen ice pack. With Rainer interpreting she tells me to sit and to tie the Ice pack to my leg with the towel. I do and it feels great. But will it be enough?

She then goes into the back room returns with the Spanish version of super glue and proceeds to fix my sunglasses. She puts them behind the counter and says, "mañana". Amazing.

I sit there for the next two hours and every twenty minutes like clockwork without saying a word, Loli (pronounced Low-lee) brings me another frozen ice pack. When it's time to close she hands me another ice pack and a small box with a tube of cream in it and tells me "tonight and mañana". I do as she instructs.

I apply the cream twice during the night because I can't sleep. I must leave early to have any chance to finish twenty miles. I only hope I can walk. Limping twenty miles does not sound like a good option.

When I go to breakfast Loli is on duty and brings me an ice pack and cafe con-leche. I'm not sure how it will hold up but I think I have a chance. I would have had no chance without Loli. She is my most recent blessing.

As I prepare to leave she wishes me Buen Camino, hands me another ice pack and tells me to put it in the ice at the next hotel (her young assistant interprets) and use it again and then gives me the cream, a card she has signed and written something on and makes the sign of the cross. I now know I can make it. These people are nice!

I could have stayed at the Albergue because it was already paid for but the truth is the comfort of a private room with a bath and the added value of having a much better chance of having access to the ice I so desperately need right now is critical. The price does not matter because I have no doubt that the value of this expense or fee is indisputable. "Price only matters in the absence of value". I believe it; I have preached it in the business for more than thirty years.

Just one month ago I played in a small event to help raise some money for a young guy and afterwards I was having a glass of wine with a friend from the Club, Rudy. The conversation is about sales and I share with Rudy my "price only matters in the absence of value" belief and he just loves it. He writes it down as if he just discovered electricity.

Rudy gets it because he is a very talented salesman. He could sell snow blowers in Miami! Price only matters in the absence of value and the small price I paid to make the change which brought me to Loli saved my Camino. I can't put a price on that!

It is 8:30 and I start. It's cold. Not chilly it's cold. There is a breeze as I start and I am not limping like I was at the end of yesterday. This will be a long day. I will walk and limp alone on my way to Astorga. My first stop will be about four miles from the starting point where I will get something to eat. I will need more than just the usual morning carb fix.

My first two miles are alongside a road. The path is narrow and with my leg still very sore I must be very careful today, even more than any other day because one miss step on a stone and I will turn an ankle and be done for. Add to the fact that I just don't know how the leg will hold up on the longest walking day of my Camino.

I make it to the cafe; Rainer is sitting outside having a little breakfast. I join him. We will walk apart because my pace will be very controlled. We will meet for dinner. Dinner will be late because with a walk of twenty miles I have no idea how long it will take. Perhaps ten hours, assuming all goes well? I don't know I have never walked this far before in a single session with 23 pounds on two good legs and today I only have one.

I have an omelet and a cafe, water and a diet coke. I finish breakfast with Swiss dark chocolate. I also buy an orange for later and an extra bottle of water. There will be a few other chances for water but I have to be sure I have enough. The weight will just have to be dealt with.

The landscape is exactly the same as the last three days. I could take a picture today and post it as four days ago and it would not matter. There will be very few pictures taken today. The real reason for a lack of interest in the scenery is the trail and the rocks and stones. They are everywhere. My poles will get a good workout today. I will spend the next six hours staring at the ground trying to avoid that one rock which will turn an ankle and create a nightmare.

I have only seen a few pilgrims today but with only one or two exceptions everyone is wounded. I pass a woman limping badly with poles in hand but no backpack. She must have sent the backpack ahead with a donkey service. She is a trooper. I am passing her and I just tell her to hang in there and she thanks me and I move on.

I'm doing okay and my leg is starting to feel the effects of the long walk. I do come close on several rocks but I avoid a big mistake. I have no idea how far I am from Astorga but I know that with each step I am getting closer.

One thing I am doing is concentrating on listening to my walk. It's strange but with the poles smashing into the ground I can take my mind off the discomfort. I'm listening to my Camino. With each step the poles record the journey. Sounds strange but it is helping.

I finally see a sign which tells me I am about four miles from Astorga. I'm going to make it but I am limping more noticeably, there are hills today and they are all tougher than they should be, especially downhill. I make it to the city. I should have about a mile to go. My leg is now worse than at any time in the last two days. I am moving like that young woman I saw hours ago. I see a sign for my hotel, I am close.

The last challenge is climbing the 84 stairs to the top where the hotel is waiting. I know its 84 because I count them. It's another way of just not focusing on what I am feeling. I make it and enter the hotel. I dump the backpack and present my passport. I am at the wrong hotel!

There are two hotels with nearly identical names. The young guy at the desk tells me it happens often. I can see by the look on his face that he can tell I don't have a lot of energy left to go much more. Good news the hotel I am in is just a five minute walk. A five minute walk is like another two miles for me right now. He shows me on a small map where I need to go.

It is a short walk. I made it! Eight and a half hours of walking and limping and I will soon be able to shower, rest and most importantly get ice!

That's it for now. Tomorrow is just thirteen and a half miles. I hope I can recover. Wish me luck.

Sunday, June 9, 2013
My Camino credential is missing....Without it no Compostela in Santiago.

I have left Astorga. I am a mile and a half into my 13 mile walk today, stage 23. I will stop at this beautiful little Church on the Camino. It is the pilgrims Church. I remove my backpack and hat and I enter the church. An elderly lady greets me and asks me to sign the Camino pilgrim's book. You are asked to write your name, the country you are from and if you are male or female. I sign in. I am visiting to take care of some personal business.

I received an email this morning from a friend at the Club who has asked me to include the brother of another friend at the Club. His 60 year old brother is fighting a difficult battle with Cancer. Gladly. He is now on my list.

I attend to my business and will now be on my way to Rabanal del Camino, a walk of 13 miles. I make my donation and the woman stops me with the Church's Camino stamp in her hand and asks me for my credential. I grab my backpack and go to the internal zippered compartment where I keep all of my critical papers including, cash, credit cards, my Passport and my Credential.

My Credential is not there! This is not possible; it's the only place I keep it. Where is it? I am now tearing apart my backpack and emptying everything in search of it. It's nowhere to be found. The old woman is watching me and she knows what the problem is. I am distraught to say the least. If I have lost it I will not be given my Compostela when I complete the walk in Santiago. This can't be happening.

Think; just think I am asking myself. Where can it be? Where did I last have it out? It was when I arrived at the hotel. There are always two things presented when you check in anywhere; Hotels, Hostals and Albergues, it's your US Passport and your credential to be stamped verifying your journey.

I have no choice. I must turn back and get to the hotel. It must be there, it has to be there. Before I leave I drop my backpack, my poles and once again remove my hat and I go back into the little Church. I am on my knees once again but this time I am asking for something very personal. That He helps me find my Credential.

I turn to leave and the old woman looks at me and makes the sign of the Cross. I am now headed back over the same first mile and a half. Other pilgrims are heading out and just looking at me obviously curious about my direction and the speed at which I am moving. My leg is better but this pace will not help. I don't care because as I am on my way back to the hotel I remember something I did yesterday that really scares me and I now have serious doubts that I will find it.

When I checked in yesterday after 20 miles and was completely spent I was at the front desk where I know I gave the clerk both my Passport and my Credential. At that time I was surrounded by more than a dozen blind people all of whom were at the hotel for some group function. I was being nudged, bumped into and otherwise rushed to get out of there as quickly as possible. In that confusion did I just put the Credential in one of my pants pockets?

This is why I am so convinced that it will not be found. When I arrived in Astorga and was limping to my hotel I passed a small version of an REI outdoor gear place and decided that after I iced my leg I would walk back that short 300 feet and replace a few things that had reached their useful end, including the pants I was wearing.

I did go to that shop in spite of my leg because it was Saturday and they would not be open on Sunday. It had to be done before they closed. I showered, iced my leg for an hour and limped back to the shop. I got there just before they were going to close. I bought new pants and a new shirt. When I left the hotel today I left the old pants behind in the trash! I was finished with them.

You cannot imagine what was going through my head as I raced back to the hotel. My 500 mile journey would be unofficial. All this work and no Compostela! How could I have been so foolish with one of my critical items?

I reach the hotel and desperately explain to the clerk what has happened, including the pants being left in the room. She completely gets the magnitude of my problem and on a hand held devise calls the cleaning people on the third floor. They have already cleaned my room but they are still on the third floor. I race to the elevator while she watches my gear. She calls the maids and lets them know that I am on my way.

When I get off the elevator two women are going through the trash and they find the pants. The woman holding the pants hands them to me. They are cargo pants with lots of pockets. I frantically search every pocket while they are dumping the contents of the plastic bag on the floor right there in the hallway.

Nothing! There is nothing in the pants or the trash. One woman hands me her key to the rooms and I head for room 310. It has to be there. It must be there. They follow me and we all search the room, moving furniture, looking under everything in the room.

Nothing. It's gone. I have lost my Credential with all of the stamps I have collected for twenty three days. I thank them for trying to help me. They understand what is missing and are honestly upset.

I return to the front desk and tell the clerk that I cannot find it. She has called yesterday's clerk and they are sure it was not left at the desk. I understand because they completely know what the Credential means and if they had found it they would have put it away in a safe place. It's gone.

I ask if I can leave everything there. "Yes", and I am out the door now headed to the gear shop desperately hoping I somehow left it there. I do take all of my critical documents that are always together in a zip lock whenever I leave the hotel. They are never out of my possession. I did use my credit card in the shop, it's my last hope.

When I get there it's as I had assumed but hoped I would be wrong about. The shop is closed, its Sunday. I walk back to the hotel no longer in any hurry just thinking about what has happened. A nightmare.

When I get back to the front desk the clerk is clearly aware of what's taking place. Desperate I empty all of my gear in the lobby and begin checking again. Every pocket of anything with a pocket. My shaving kit. Nothing.

There is a small pocket on the inside of my backpack which cannot be seen and in it I have only two items which have not been touched since I got on the plane to Madrid on May 13th. A card that Robin gave me with a letter and instructions on the envelope to not open until I was on the plane. Another card from Amanda with instructions not to open until day number 30, it's not yet open.

When I reach into this pocket that you cannot see, my Credential is in there. I have found it! I cannot explain how it is possible for my Credential to be there. I cannot. I show it to the clerk and she is as happy as I am and offers to make me a photocopy. I just hand it to her. She returns and has copied it and taped the pieces together. She tells me to keep them away from the original. Which I will do.

I am exhausted from the last hour and a half but more thrilled that my nightmare is over. I return to the Camino and I go directly back to the little Church. The old woman sees me come back into the Church and I hand her my Credential, she just smiles and stamps it.

I return to the same pew, I have some business to attend to. I will end here and in the next segment I will go back and complete my day in Astorga before I bring my blog up to date about my 13 mile walk. Sorry, make that my 16 mile walk to complete stage 23. It just keeps getting better. Good night.

Monday, June 10, 2013
Stage 24...The 13 mile walk I turn into...16 miles....But first let me introduce you to Irish Ann.

I gave her that name because it's short for ANNoying. Before my walk to Rabanal I will first bring you up to date on just a couple of things. First, while in Astorga Rainer and I bump into Burgos Ray in the plaza near the Cathedral on our way to dinner. We stop to chat. Burgos Ray is a really nice guy.

I congratulate him for continuing on. When I last saw him he was stopping short of our destination by about six mikes so I thought that given his struggles, he would catch up.

He and Rainer are speaking to each other in German briefly and then he wishes me well on my Camino. We move on. Rainer tells me that in their brief conversation that Burgos Ray has taken the donkey service to get here and that he will be going by donkey service to Santiago tomorrow from here. He is giving up his Camino.

Rainer goes on to tell me that Burgos Ray said that he was home sick and made a mistake by trying to walk the Camino without being prepared. I can understand that. Perhaps he will try again.

We will first stop at a Cafe near the restaurant we are going to because it's too early. The name of the restaurant is Restaurante

Serrano. Rainer and I pull up a stool and order a glass of wine when Irish Ann arrives and pulls up a stool between us. First a little history.

Back in Mansilla, stage 21 was when I first met Irish Ann. I simply forgot about her and that's not easy to do. It was after dinner and Rainer, Michele and Emma and I are having a beer getting ready to call it a night. This woman, Irish Ann just barges into our conversation and latches on to us. She orders a beer and begins her Q&A.

She asks me where I am from and I tell her California. That information immediately causes her to begin a speech about our current political structure. I interrupted her and told her that I would not have this conversation or any other political conversation because I would not allow that to damage my Camino experience. She presses on.

BC Jim would have handled this situation very differently. I choose to be AC Jim. I push my beer away and say good night to all and I leave. It's late and I need to rest. Irish Ann has provided me with an exit strategy. She is just annoying

I have not seen her again until she pushes her stool between Rainer and me here in Astorga. BC Jim is about to make an appearance. I said "excuse me; you are not joining us uninvited in an attempt to drag me into a political conversation. When I last saw you I politely asked you to stop and you ignored me. I am not going to allow that to happen again". I turn to Rainer and simply say "let's go to dinner". He smiles, we abandon our $2 glass of wine and we leave. Another good decision. Irish Ann has no idea just how close she was to meeting BC Jim at a much different level.

Restaurante Serrano is a family business. The Chef is the son, the head waiter is his sister, Mom is also in the kitchen and Dad runs the cash register. The son owns the Restaurant. I will not be able to go through the entire experience so I will just say that it is the best Restaurant I have been to in years. Not just the Camino, anywhere.

I like good food and wine. I just walked 20 miles and I would do it again if at the end I would get to eat here. It was that good! Pat and John this is a must on the list. Just a note for Pat and John, visit the Bierzo wine region.

The next morning before my nightmare with my Credential I have coffee and toast. I am up late and I leave at 11:00. I think it's because the bed is so comfortable I am in no rush. Why bother its only thirteen miles.

Fast forward to being back on the Camino. The weather is very nice. I bit cool and a little breeze. The walk today will be flat until the final two miles. My leg is sore but if I go easy I think it will be ok. The first cafe away from the city is about two and a half miles. Add to that my extra three miles and by the time I get there I need something to eat.

MESON EL LLAR. Wow, it just keeps getting better. I have taken pictures which Robin may post. Simply stated this is wonderful. Pat and John skip the carb breakfast in Astorga and start your day here.

The balance of the walk is uneventful which is good. I even take a few pictures and I stopped a couple of times, remove the limos, put on some of Lilo's cream and go slow. The last two miles is all up hill and it does cause some limping. I will fix that with ice.

I will have a simple salad and a small dish of pasta. The food is pilgrim food. Not Serrano's. I eat alone. Rainer decided to stay in Astorga and will catch up in a couple of days by donkey. I have my ice and it's an early night. It's been a very long day but all is good.

My leg is improving, I have my Credential and tomorrow stage 25 is a walk of sixteen and a half miles to Molinaseca.

Good night.

Monday, June 10, 2013
Stage 25 17 miles to Molinaseca...A closer look at the map would have given me a warning, this will be difficult.

I am awake early, it's Monday June 10th. At least I think it's the tenth. I received a message about my last post which makes me think it was not posted, so I just sent it. I hope it's not a duplicate.

On to Molinaseca. What I would have seen had I looked more closely at my guidebook this morning is that there will be significant elevation changes leaving Rabanal. The climb will be about seven hundred feet and the terrain will be rough trails almost always covered in rocks, lots of rocks.

First a little update on my equipment. I have now lost two pairs of sunglasses and I have had two additional pair lost to damage. The pair that Loli fixed for me did not make it. Even Spanish super glue could not save my seven Euro bargain glasses. The forth pair to end in the trash were purchased on Saturday at the gear shop. Loli's repaired glasses were starting to show signs of failure so I bought this fourth pair just in case. I was correct so that when Loli's fell apart I was ready. I paid twenty two Euros for this beautiful pair. They lasted one day falling victim to the Camino when I dropped them on a rock while taking a break. Stage 25 will be without glasses for about twelve miles. A new pair at the end of stage twenty five will put the count to five pair for those keeping score.

Back to the start of this day.

I am packing and before I will leave for the morning's toast choices I check my email. There are several. All good, friends just checking in and sending kind words about hanging in there and to keep using the ice—all helpful and motivating comments, but there is also one from one of the old sales team which makes my day.

It's from Larry and he says keep the ice going and good luck and then he goes on to say that he really enjoyed the Price only matters. He said "I remember when you started our meeting with this opening line "Does everyone here know that Kmart sells men's suits?" I laughed. I do remember that presentation. "Two pairs of slacks, a shirt, a tie and a reversible vest all for just $89.99". Why would you buy a suit anywhere else?" You know where the presentation goes from here. That was fun.

Fun. Business and fun. Charles always said that the business is not supposed to be fun, it should be rewarding and that can be on many levels but not fun. Speaking of Charles I think now is as good a time as any to explain, as I had promised, where BC Jim and AC Jim came from.

When I was first asked to rebuild the business, I knew that what was needed was a complete remodel. I mean everything. Most importantly

I had to find the right people and that would mean that nearly the entire group of existing people would have to go.

What will also be needed is a very direct style of management. One way or the highway. I was good at that. My nickname soon became Simon as in the guy from American Idol. I took that as a compliment. I could be downright brutal. Ever fired someone in a meeting with 300 people there? I did. Not the best way to handle it but I can tell you it was effective.

Fast forward to three years later. Our business is booming I have great people; our growth is getting lots of attention. But there is a problem. You cannot keep growing without change. What I needed was someone who could help us change our culture, including me. I needed to make that change so that all of the people in the business could improve and develop. People, you must have the right people.

There was a very talented guy working in the headquarters office that had the ear of the Chairman and was responsible for Global Executive Development. I saw him facilitate two management meetings and I knew I needed to hire him.

There is a process you must follow when moving people from one unit to another, you know, rules. I skipped all of that, I had dinner with Charles in Philadelphia and made him an offer he could not refuse. He said yes.

There were a lot of people upset with me. Take a number. I knew I was right and three years later I proved it. As a matter of fact Charles and I were asked to give a presentation to the Management Team on how we implemented our changes.

Charles began the work of changing the culture in our business unit and all of our people grew. In addition Charles got me to change. No more firings at meetings, no more razor sharp comments or letters to my peers and the list goes on.

Jim before Charles (BC Jim) Jim after Charles (AC Jim). I do my best to stay in AC mode but I can tell you that BC Jim still makes an appearance once in a while. I made a lot of great hires in more than thirty years, Charles was one of them.

Speaking of great people—Happy Birthday, Maggie, my Executive Assistant for ten years. And in spite of what Charles said we had some fun. Maggie would agree.

I start on my stage 25 in cooler temperatures. Its 9:00 am, plenty of time to go slow. My leg is better and if I am careful and take more breaks, it will reduce the stress. I estimate that I should reach my final destination by 4:00 leaving time for my gear and a nice break before dinner.

I could not have been more wrong. I find out quickly that I will be tested today and it will last for the entire 17 miles. As soon as I start, the walk is straight up hill about six hundred and fifty feet. Not really hard but it comes early and I am sore. Throw in the rocks and I am no longer thinking about a nice break before dinner. I am stopping for water more often and I am consuming it quickly. I will need to resupply at the first location available, that's about three miles away.

When I reach that point I get two bottles of water and some fruit. I need to sit and look at the map in the guide book. When I do, I realize that this day is not going to be like those last three days, long and flat.

I am looking at the map and I will soon be at the top and will then head down about three hundred feet and then back to the top. The real test won't start until about the seven mile mark and then it gets serious. From that point on for the last ten miles I will be crawling down the mountain for about twenty seven hundred feet!

I am moving as best I can when the terrain lets me. At the top the views are spectacular. I take some pictures because when I do I am also giving my left leg a break. My right leg is fine but now my shoulders are feeling it. And a new entry in the soreness group, my hands.

Holding on to the poles for more than three hundred and fifty miles while slamming them into the cement like ground and dealing with the rocks has finally shown up.

There isn't a great deal more to say about today. It's just very hard. I finish my walk to Molinaseca in eight and a half hours. Today has been the third most difficult day. I have one more test ahead of me. It is the one that everyone has been talking about for the last two weeks because it is commonly said to be the second toughest day. That will be my stage 27 which I will face on Wednesday. There will be two six hundred feet changes. First up and then back down before facing the last physical test, a climb of twenty four hundred feet to the top.

One small problem about Wednesdays walk, I have one before it on Tuesday. Tuesday's walk will be nineteen miles. I need some rest, I'm sore from head to toe. Good night.

Tuesday, June 11, 2013
Stage 26...Nineteen miles plus detour for a total of twenty one...My second secret weapon...The Mall.

Nineteen miles I turn into twenty one on my way to Villafranca del Bierzo.

First, my arrival in Molinaseca, the end of stage 25. It was a very tough day. As I said already, it was the third most difficult day thus far.

I make it to Molinaseca; it took me nearly nine hours. I am beat and now searching for my hotel. The last thing I want to do is to walk past it and have to double back, there is just something about covering the same ground twice.

As I enter this small village I cross over a bridge and I spot a Farmacia. I will stop there, buy something and ask for directions to the Muriel. I walk in and the first thing I see is a sunglasses display. Perfect, I need another pair. I buy them and ask for directions. I am very close, just a couple of hundred yards to the left and I will soon be in the shower. I find it, it was very close.

I check in and take care of all of the paperwork with Javier. He shows me to my room, 102. It's on the third floor. Don't ask I don't have a clue as to how room 102 is on the third floor. All I know is that after I climb to the third floor I will done for the day.

Javier opens the door and it's the smallest room to date. I don't care. I completely dump my backpack and get the Veep working and then the shower. It's now about 7:00 and I do want something to eat, but

I have no interest in a pilgrim's dinner that is not served until 8:30. I head back down stairs in search of something simple and quick. I need to get back to my mini suite to ice my left leg.

As I leave the hotel I immediately spot a small market. I will need some things for tomorrow so I should take care of that now while it's still open. As I enter the owner hands me a piece of ham he has just sliced. It's fantastic. I don't know what it's called and I don't care. I ask him to slice more. He understands and I continue to look around for snacks to take with me. It's the owner again and this time he has sliced a piece of cheese and hands it to me. It's delicious. Pease slice more. I am now putting together something I can bring back to my room and eat while icing my leg. This is starting to come together. I buy a bag of chips, a sinkers and three bottles of water, con gas.

I am back at the hotel in less than thirty minutes. Javier is at the desk. I ask for a glass of Crienza Riojia. While he is opening the wine I ask him if there might be a bigger room available. He understands and says yes! It's room 103, right next door to my mini suite. Off we go. I have my dinner and wine with me as we climb back to see room 103.

He opens the door to 103 and it looks like a suite at the Plaza compared to 102. I'll take it. How much? Ten Euro extra. Price only matters….

I get my leg squared away and my dinner is ready and I am starting to recover. I will check my email and finish my blog for the day. I never took a sip of the wine. The Wi-Fi does not work in 103 and the last thing I'm going to do is to go back down three flights to ask why.

I fall sleep, I think around 8:30 and wake up again at 2:30 in the morning. My leg is still wrapped in ice although the ice has melted a great deal. My leg does not seem much better. I remove the ice and go to the Spanish Bengay. I start to write my blog and a couple of emails which I will try to send from the cafe in the morning. Hopefully the Wi-Fi will work from there. For the first time since arriving in Spain on May 14th I set the alarm on my iPhone. I cannot afford to sleep late I have nineteen miles to face and will need an early start. I set it for 7:00 am with a goal of being on the Camino by 8:30.

The alarm wakes me at 7:00. It's time to pack, have a carb fest and get on with my nineteen mile journey. I am on schedule, packed most everything and I will head to breakfast. Before I leave my suite 103 on the third floor I do realize that I am missing a pair of socks. They must be in junior 102. No problem Javier will help fix the problem.

I get to the cafe and tell Javier that I have left something in room 102 and he gives me the key. I sit and wait for my breakfast. It gives me a chance to see if the Wi-Fi works in the cafe. It does and I start to receive emails.

I get several emails, all wishing me well and to just keep using the ice. All of this advice and encouragement is helpful. I also get one that is both funny and expected. It's from Mike. We play a lot of golf together and Mike always drives the cart. He drives for three reasons: 1) because he keeps score 2) because he has never lost a golf cart and 3) Mike was a professional race car driver.

His email is perfectly timed. He sends a message about me having to buy my fifth pair of sun glasses. He knows me like a book.

What's funny is that as I receive Mike's email I am on my way to get my missing socks in 102 which I left behind in haste to get to my new room, get the ice started and have a bite to eat. Back up the stairs and I have the key for 102.

I enter 102 and begin the search. No socks but I did find my poles, foot cream, my water bottle and my micro fiber towel! I guess it was good that the socks were missing. I return to 103.

I am ready to leave and I pick up my jacket and there are the socks. Now I do have everything and I am on my way to today's nineteen mile test. Mike would understand.

The weather is good. It's a bit cool but the sky is clear and there isn't much wind. My leg is acting up and it feels weaker than it has in the last two days. I'm beginning to think that the ice has a positive effect for a period of time and then perhaps I should apply heat. I'm not sure but I am concerned with what I'm feeling and where I am going. I just need to deal with it. At this moment I remember a very special phone call I had with one of my best sales people many years ago.

As our business grew much larger I was becoming further removed from the point of sale. With more than one hundred sales people in the field it happens. I would see my top performers a few times each year and they would call from time to time. I enjoyed the phone contact because it kept me closer to what was going on at point of sale. If you had sales of more than $100 million each year you could call me anytime. If your sales were less than $100 million each year, call at your own risk, BC Jim might pick up the phone.

I got a call from one of my very best sales people and this is what took place. The caller is one of my top ten producers, an elite group of talented people. He was young as we're many of them and he was still learning and developing.

He began the call by immediately complaining about a service issue involving one large piece of business. He was very angry and offered solutions including a couple of terminations and other drastic steps. I just listened. He finally reached the point where he was repeating himself when I asked "are you done"? A quiet response, "yes".

"Now it's my turn. I am going to give you something to do today. You will cancel all of your other work until you have completed this assignment, I will not accept any excuse for failing to do what I tell you to do".

"When I end this call you will go to the Mall, buy yourself a cup of coffee and find a bench to sit on. You will stay there until you see a young mother or a couple walk past you with a child that clearly has a lifelong disability and then you will call me back and we will finish this conversation. Do you understand"?

I got a very subdued "yes" and I hang up.

Later that day he called me back. I took the call. All he said was "Jim I apologize, I am sorry; I will never call you again with a single complaint. I get it".

"Good, now get back to work and don't ever forget what you just told me". I had forgotten that story although I have told it to a number of young managers as part of my coaching. And because of that memory I will not be writing about my left leg and or any other "minor problem I think I may have".

When I start to think its tough and or that this or that is bothering me I will just tell myself to remember The Mall. This is my new, second secret weapon. It's one we can all use.

I finished the first four miles in very good time. My leg is not a problem. I take my first rest stop. I have a little water, a Snickers and a couple of cherries which I bought last night at the market. This is the Camino snack package. At the start of today's walk there are flat paved roads and walkways giving my left leg a much needed break. I have come to the conclusion that for me the length of the walk is not the challenge, for me it's the surface of the trail.

Walking yesterday up and down very steep hills with lots of rocks was very difficult. Just trying to avoid one small injury is the entire focus. I would prefer a walk of twenty miles on a good surface than a walk of ten miles on a trail like yesterday's trail.

The views are quite impressive but I must stop to see them. I am just walking with my eyes completely glued to the trail. At one point that approach came in handy as I miss stepping on about a two and a half foot snake. I step to the right, stop and take a picture of my new friend. I sent it to Robin. I have no idea what kind it is and I really don't care. As my good friend Bill at Desert Mountain says, "I don't like any creatures that don't have shoulders". Me too.

Speaking of creatures, I am passing through a very small village and I am greeted by three dogs all very aggressive and running directly at me. This is where the poles are a good investment. One of the three is getting much to close and acting like he will take a bite out of me. I keep moving but I get very aggressive with the poles and that's as close as they get. The real problem is that I was hoping to find a place with shade to take a break. The dogs have killed that idea as they chase me out of town,

The weather is fine it's just starting to warm up. By the time I reach Villafranca del Bierzo it will be in the mid 80's.

I made it! It took more than eight and a half hours. I just need to find my hotel and get in the shower, ice my leg and rest before dinner. As I noted in my previous blog Stage 27, a long walk of more than 18 miles with significant elevation change and an even more difficult descent awaits me tomorrow. By the way when I start Stage 27 tomorrow I will have the same number of days remaining to walk as there are letters in Santiago, eight!

Did you notice that I did not go into any of the details about my "detour"? What's the point? I missed a turn and had to go back. Probably added two miles, but who's complaining? Not me, I'm thinking about The Mall right now.

Good night.

Thursday, June 13, 2013
This will be a Stage 26 update...My detour, its complex. It's embarrassing and it will be one of my most memorable days.

I purposely did not go into any details about my "detour" in stage 26 because it warrants its own full post. I think you will agree.

I could not include the details because it would have taken me a great deal of time to tell you what happened. I was tired, really tired when I finally reached Villafranca. I was not just physically tired but more mentally spent—almost as much as I was on the Credential day. I said it was no big deal but it was actually monumental! So here is what actually happened yesterday.

I am going along at a very good pace; my leg after the first mile was as good as it was before I injured it. Yes, I was back to nearly full strength. That's good but it will come back and cause a huge problem.

I am about nine miles into Stage 26, or so I think. As it turns out I am a couple of miles ahead of that. This will now create a detour that may be a record. I am at a fork in the trail and I have a problem. Most of the Camino markings are stationary and permanent. You will see the Camino shell or more often than not you will see a hand painted yellow arrow directing you.

At times there will be yellow arrows on buildings, street signs, curbs, trees and lots of other permanent structures. But there are also these printed signs with the yellow arrow which have been produced on what looks like a twelve by twelve piece of Styrofoam. They are not permanent. They are just set out leaning on a wall or any number of on other permanganate objects. Making sense?

Well at this fork in the road there are actually three different trails all going off in different directions and the Styrofoam marker is just sitting on top of a bush obviously put there by the wind or the rain. It's pointing straight up. No direction. I stop, take off my backpack and get out my guide book to look at the map. There are zero reference points where I am standing. No other pilgrims can be seen in any direction. None and I need to make a decision.

What I don't know is that I have long passed where I think I am and based on that the map says I need to go left. So I go left. What will happen may be a Camino record for a "detour" taken by a pilgrim. Are you starting to see why I left this out yesterday? In addition to the time it would take explain what happened, I am going to dinner and I want to complete the basic Stage 26 blog. I can›t do it after dinner because it will be too late and I need to leave early to face what will become my toughest day. That will be covered in my Stage 27 blog. I just completed stage 27 and it took me more than eleven hours! That's for later.

Back to my detour. I walk more than ten miles on my "detour" but of course I have no idea what has happened. I pass through a forest for more than two hours being attacked by all sorts of bugs. I pull up my neck scarf over the back of my head and my hat and I pull up the front up to my eyes. The net result is that I am now experiencing what it must be like looking out of a Gurkha. It's weird. What happens next will make this day my number two most memorable, second only to my Credential day. That cannot be topped even by this.

Are you starting to understand why I left this out yesterday? Well the best is yet to come.

I finally come out of the forest and see daylight for the first time in more than an hour. I know something is terribly wrong. I come to a small village. I have been walking down hill for a long time. The village is empty of people but there are a lot of cats. I reach a main road and stop to look at the map. There is a sign that says I am in

San Juan something or other and I cannot find it anywhere on my maps. Nothing and this is not good. Now which way to go? If left back there was wrong I will now go right. I don't have much choice.

I walk about a half a mile. I have been walking for nearly eight hours. Up ahead there is a fairly large building with a large sign that says BAR. There are lots of cars in the parking lot. I will go there and try to get directions.

As I walk across the road I see two guys talking in the parking lot. I actually ask in Spanish, "question, please" and they both just look at me while I hand the younger big guy my iPad Mimi with the address of my hotel in Villafranca and the guy goes nuts! He's waving his hands all over the place speaking to the older guy in Spanish at eighty words a minute. I sense this is not good. I don't understand a word he is saying while the older guy is speaking to me at an even faster rate. I wait for an opening and I simply ask "kilometers". The young guy says a number I think I understand but I can't believe it. The older guy is agreeing with him as he continues to wave his hands all over the place. Are you sitting down?

He tells me that I am 40 kilometers from Villafranca! That's farther away than when I first started eight hours ago. I am, to put it mildly, stunned! I'm speechless, completely speechless. My next one word question is simply "taxi" and they both go back into crazy mode saying only, "no, no, no".

I make that universal hand signal for telephone and they both just say "no". I get it; there is no taxi service here, in wherever it is I am standing. I reach in my pocket and take out every Euro I have, 75. Remember when I first left Javier's hotel and tried the

ATM? Technical Difficulties? That's all I have 75 Euros. They both continue their rapid fire conversation as they turn and head for the bar. I am in shock. Its 4:00 and I am twenty miles away from Villafranca.

I need to think of a solution. This is not a good time to panic. Starting to see why this was not part of yesterday's blog?

I am tired, I need to sit and think. I follow them into the bar. I open the door and it's a mad house of men screaming from one end of this very large room to the other. There are several card games in progress. I don't know what games they are playing but it appears that in order to play you must scream a lot at each other. No one notices that I have walked in. It takes a while but I finally get a beer and head back to the front porch which is completely empty and I sit at a little table where I know that I must figure something out. This is just incredible.

I am sitting there for about fifteen minutes while men come and go. It's like I am invisible and then out comes the old guy I first met in the parking lot. He starts speaking to me in Spanish and he can tell I don't understand him. He stops talking and points at me, then points at himself and makes a gesture like he is driving a car! I think he is saying that he will drive me to Villafranca! He then points at his watch which I think is him telling me when he can leave. He goes back inside. Did I misunderstand him? Is he going to give me a ride? I am not sure but I am hoping I am correct.

At 4:45 the older guy and the big young guy come out of the bar and wave at me to follow them to the older guy's car. Its looks exactly like the car that Peter Sellers drove in the movie the Pink Panther. I put my backpack and poles in the back, the old guy is driving, the young guy is in the back seat and I am in the front passenger seat. We start and the old guy points at my seatbelt. I understand.

So here I am in the Pink Panther car driving on a freeway at about 50 miles an hour with two complete strangers who I can't communicate with going I don't know where. I ask the young guy, in Spanish, his name. He tells me Jose. The old guy says the same, Jose. The young guy tells me that it's Duos Jose's and that the older guy is his father. Jose and Jose junior.

We arrive in Villafranca in about twenty minutes. The son was correct, about twenty miles. I am in Villafranca. They both get out and in their own way I can tell they are happy for me. I offer the 75 Euros and they say "no". I insist and the son takes it.

They drive away and two hours later I am regretting that in all of the thank you I can say to them, I wish I had taken their picture. Now you know why I did not want to try and add this to the Stage 26 blog.

In summary I should have turned right and walked about eight miles to Villafranca but I turned left and walked about them miles to the bar in San Juan something resulting in the nearly twenty mile "detour".

I have now been transferred twice by four complete strangers just trying to help me on my Camino. Two policemen in a patrol car with lights on the roof and two men named Jose in a Peter Seller's Pink Panther car without lights on the roof!

This will be my second most memorable day on the Camino. I am exhausted. I will post my Stage 27 journey tomorrow.

Before I go I do want to tell you that today was the toughest day I have had thus far and that I did not leave anything at my last hotel and I did not take any "detours" today!

Good night.

Thursday, June 13, 2013
Stage 27...Up and over the mountain...By far my toughest day...Even tougher than my snow day.

At the end of Stage 26 I am meeting Rainer for dinner at the hotel. Dinner will start late, at 9:00 and I don't mind because after what I experienced with my "detour" I need to just regroup mentally as well as needing some rest. I get my gear taken care of and a shower. I have about two hours to myself.

I set the alarm on my iPhone just in case I fall asleep while trying to get the day's blog written. Trying to put the day together mentally is not going to happen which leads to the decision to separate the "detour" from the rest of the day.

As I am going through the gear I decide that at least two pieces of clothing will be left behind in order to reduce weight for Stage 27. Not difficult given the fact that all of it is shot.

Dinner is good but not great. I have the duck but it's not cooked enough. I won't send it back, it's just not important, I'm not very hungry. The wine is good and we are now in the Bierzo region. Rainer came here by bus and has not decided if he will walk Stage 27.

I don't tell him about the "detour", it's too embarrassing and the details would leave little time for any other topics. We do discuss my upcoming task which I will complete during my last seven days, Stages 28-34. I will tell you what that is after I complete Stage 28. I have been planning it since I was in training.

I meet Rainer for breakfast. I need to go over Stage 27 the destination, O'Cebreiro in detail. There are three routes to choose from to get over the mountain. They all will require the last five mile elevation challenge and I don't want a repeat of the "minor" error I made in Stage 26. I am a bit nervous about having three route choices, but I'm confident that Rainer will know what's best.

He has prepared a written note which gives me nine checks points. He has included the distance between each in kilometers. I can just keep it in my pocket. He shows me the route in my book. We finish breakfast. Rainer is taking his time and has decided to go ahead to Triacastela by bus because he can't find a hotel in O'Cebreiro. Triacastela is the Stage 28 destination on Thursday.

The first ten miles of Stage 27 are fairly flat and on a solid surface mostly paved road through small villages (the check points) which gives me plenty of opportunity to stop, rest and keep up the water supply. I will need it, it's getting very warm. Rainer told me at breakfast that the temperature today will be as high as 29 C which I know is very warm. I really do need to figure out the C math.

I do stop several times because I know what's ahead. I will soon find out that I really don't know just how very, very difficult it will be. When I do stop I am now really taking breaks including taking off my Limos and even undressing the passengers. It's all okay because everyone does it, it's the Camino.

At one of my last check points I have my pre-climb the Mountain meal. Keep in mind that these little places are just mostly snacks shops. Here it is: a Diet Coke, a banana, a small donut, a Snickers and a glass of freshly squeezed orange juice. How's that for a power lunch.

I have now walked for about eight miles and I think I can see it, the Mountain, hard to be sure but I am starting to get a sense of what is coming.

I have seen a growing number of pilgrims today on this route; many of them are limping and I will see less and less of them as the climb starts. Two distinct memories will stay with me at the end of Stage 27. The first is the number of times I was sure I had reached the top and would quickly realize that I had not. I can't tell you how many times I thought it was over but it's more than eight or nine times. I just stopped counting. Nothing more disappointing than thinking you are there and you are not only wrong but what is in front of you around a hidden corner is another piece of the hill that is steeper and its rock covered surface is worse. My poles are working very hard and my hands are feeling it.

The second memory I will keep from Stage 27 is the Bull. Yes the bull. I not only have pictures, I have a video. As I am climbing yet another hill I did not think existed, I look up and coming directly at me from the top of the hill and completely taking up the entire trail is a herd of cows, all very large and all with horns. There is also a bull. He is big and his color is black, the cows are all brown and or tan. I have to find a place to get out of the way. I climb up the bank on the side of the trail and find just enough room to get out of the way or I hope it's enough room.

The herd is being lead down the mountain by an old man with a very long stick and three dogs. His horses are just walking behind him and the herd. As they pass me they are not more than arms-length from me. The bull just slowly passes and he gives me a glance. The video is quite good. I will send pictures to Robin.

Speaking of pictures I do take some of the view from the top. It's the reward. In the end it takes me nearly eleven hours to complete Stage 27. I get to my room and as fast as I can I am in the shower. There will be no need for Veep today. I will throw away everything I was wearing. I have completely sweated through it all. Even Veep in a machine is no match. I will buy a tee shirt and find some replacements as soon as possible.

I am not very hungry but I go to the cafe where I sit and have a large salad and ice my leg while eating. It's quite common. Hard to believe but in just one hour after that brutal walk I'm recovered and feel good. Just a little ice and some Spanish leg cream and I will be ready for Stage 28, a walk to Triacastela just 13.2 miles but all downhill and with little shade.

Another detour! Yes I have done it again. This error will cause me to walk an additional 3.2 miles on my most difficult day. I did not make a wrong turn. I get to the top of the final hill and I see a sign with an arrow to O'Cebbeiro. I just keep going and begin to get a bit concerned that I have done it again!

I walk slowly done a hill through the trees and I see a small building. I will stop there and find out where I am. I am exhausted. I walk into the Casa Jaime and ask for a small beer. I am the only customer. I will soon find out why. I show the young woman behind the bar my iPad and ask how much farther to O'Cebbeiro. She looks at me with a strange look and then tells me that I just walked right through and past it!

No choice, I turn around and begin the march back up the hill of about 3.1 km to my hotel. I have now added about 3.2 miles to this a very difficult day and yes I do recognize the hotel once I get there as a place I just walked right past.

Just seven more days and I will complete my Camino. I have only 96 miles in front of me. That's it. Have a nice day.

Thursday, June 13, 2013
Stage 28...down the hill a drop of two thousand feet, thirteen and a half miles to Triacastela

I am awake early. I slept well because of how much Stage 27 and the uphill climb took out of me. The good news is that it's behind me. I am now in the final Region of the Camino, Galicia. When I complete today's Stage 28 I will be six days from Santiago.

I will take my time leaving today because when I first look out the window it is raining and there is some hail. It's cold at the top of the mountain. It's very cold. I get dressed and go to have coffee early just to get outside and try to get a feel for the weather.

It's a short walk to the cafe. It's packed with pilgrims, some of whom are downright rude. There is one woman trying to keep up with all of the coffee orders. It's not possible, each cup is made individually, and it's not like the waitress at a diner who just walks around with a pot of coffee in her hand continuously offering refills. There is also one guy working and his only job is to make the toast and he can't keep up. This is madness so I will come back later.

I'm in no hurry because the weather is not good right now so I will wait it out, perhaps it will improve.

I will just go back to my "suite" and take a look at the map for today's walk and do a better job of preparing.

I also forgot to tell you about the British couple I met last night while icing my leg. John and Vivian who live outside of London I think is what they said. Nice people.

Our conversation starts with a question from John about my injury. I explain that it's just a muscle strain and that with some ice and my Spanish hot cream I will be fine. By the way I don't know what the injury really is I am just guessing but I do think that's what it is.

The conversation continues about how tough the mountain is and I am a bit surprised at how relaxed and comfortable they appear to be after such a tough day. John asks me where I began my Camino and I tell him St Jean to which he responds «that›s where we started as well, three years ago". Three years ago! Now that's what I call a "Detour", a really big detour. Maybe I'm not in the record book yet.

He explains. He and Vivian return to the Camino each year, select a section they will walk and then return home. I'm not sure but I think there is a donkey service involved. It does not matter; everyone does the Camino in whatever way fits them best.

So now I've met pilgrims on both ends of the spectrum. The Brazilian guy who will complete the Camino in just twenty four days and this English couple who will compete there's in perhaps four or five years.

I was right about the weather. At 9:30 it's vastly improved and I return for coffee and now there are only a few people. I order my coffee and toast. It's okay but not great. One thing that strikes me is the number of people who are wearing shorts. It's still pretty cold. I am still a wimp.

I am packed and on my way with everything, yes everything. I also know exactly where I am going and how I will approach today's walk. I will go slowly. I will take breaks along the way at a number of check points. I will also eat something when I reach Alto do Poio which is about four and a half miles from my starting point. I will just walk past Casa Jaime today, I don't yet need directions.

It's cold but I have dressed as well as I could for it. My hands are cold but everything else is ok. I will soon be shedding layers as the weather improves all day and it actually gets warm.

There are a number of uphill climbs and then back down again until you finally get to the last hill that brings you to Alto do Poio. The last hill to the top is a pretty steep hill and I take a couple of breaks, I'm in no hurry.

When I reach the top there is immediately on my right about thirty pilgrims sitting on the patio having something to eat or drink. This looks like a popular place, I will stop here.

When I walk inside there are a few tables and I see that a number of pilgrims are having the soup. I don't know what it is but it looks good. I order the soup. Its spinach soup with small pieces of vegetables, it's very good. I remove the Limos and give the passengers a break. I will repeat this at least three more times today. I do notice that the Limos are looking a bit tired. Just get me to Santiago, only about eighty five more miles.

The steep downhill section does not start until I am about four miles from the destination. Once it starts it will not stop until Stage 28 is completed. I just go slowly; the trail is once again covered in rocks.

I arrive without an event at 5:15. It was difficult in parts but nothing like yesterday. It's a nice little village. Take care of the gear, shower and then go to try a glass of white wine which is what Galicia is famous for.

Tomorrow, Friday June 14th will be Stage 29, a walk of only twelve miles to Sarria. Only six days to Santiago. Have a nice day.

Friday, June 14, 2013
Stage 29...On my way to Sarria...I now have only six days remaining to complete My Camino.

The walk to Askaris will be fairly easy with just a few rolling hills and only one hill of any real size. It appears that I will once again have good weather. I looked out my window and many of the pilgrims are walking in shorts and t-shirts. I will also walk in shorts and a tee shirt but not because I want to, I have no choice. It's the only outfit I have left.

Off to breakfast and I will begin to get a feel for the weather. I am wearing the shorts, tee shirt combo and my rain jacket. It's fine, this should work. I will try to find some other replacements to get me to Santiago once I arrive in Sarria.

I have my morning fix of bread, coffee and orange juice. I will need to find a Farmacia on my way to Sarria; I am almost out of sunblock.

There are two routes available today. One route is about a mile and a half shorter but there is much less shade. The second longer route, The Roman route, is longer but it is also a bit flatter and for the majority of the day there will be shade. It's already getting warm as I pack so I decide to take the Roman route. Today will be a walk of about 14 miles. When I arrive in Sarria I will then have less than eighty three miles remaining.

The first three miles is alongside a roadway. The trail and the road are separated by a substantial guard rail. This part of the trail is a solid surface, no rocks. There is shade for about half of this part and then the Camino goes through the forest. A river is on my left for the first two hours and it is running rapidly which helps drown out the sound of the nearby traffic. I will stop at the first small village to eat something and pick up some additional water. The temperature is rising making it more important to have an adequate supply of water.

The first few villages I pass through don't offer anything in the way of a cafe so I just continue on to Samos which is about six miles from today's start. The village is beautiful and as you enter the village crossing over the Rio Oribio you see this massive monastery. I stop here and take a picture. I need something to eat. There are two cafes just across the bridge and the first one appears to be crowded with pilgrims. I head to the second cafe. There are seats outside but they are all in the sun. I step inside and there are tables. The cafe is very clean and has a nice choice of smaller items that are not all engulfed in a loaf of bread. I have a salad and an agua con gas. I will also refill my metal bottle which hooks onto the front of my backpack. Perfect, back to the Camino.

As I am leaving he village I see a Farmacia and I stop to get my sunblock and realize that I also need more of the Spanish spots cream. I show the clerk my two current versions. She has the sports cream and offers a different sun screen. Fine, that was easy.

The balance of the day is just a slow walk through many villages and farms with lots of cattle and lots of dogs and cats. I have only one "event" today. No, I don't get lost or leave something behind. When I stopped at the small cafe I bought water with gas with my salad, two small bottles. When I asked the young girl to please put two bottles of cold water in my metal bottle I did not say "con gas".

Well, she put two bottles of con gas in my bottle which bounces around as I walk and sure enough it explodes just under my chin. I'm now cooled off by my water bottle and it's not a problem, it's warm and there is plenty of water ahead. It did get my attention when it started hissing just before it burst.

I will just fill the bottle myself from now on.

I arrive in Sarria at 4:15 which means my walk today took about seven hours including a number of breaks and a longer than average lunch break. No issues just a bit tired and sore. Nothing the ice and the cream can't handle.

First order of business after a shower will be to find a store for a couple of replacement items that will get me to Santiago, now just five days away. I find a shop and buy a pair of cargo shorts, two light weight shirts and I am now ready for the final five days.

I have been planning more than five months for the Sarria to Santiago final five days. I have a couple of very special tasks to complete. At the end of tomorrow's post I will share that with you.

I will ask Robin to post the picture of my four Cross's. That's it for now. Have a good day.

Sunday, June 16, 2013
Stage 30...I have a very busy day in front of me...My four Cross's, the seven stones and a card to open...All good.

Today I will walk twelve miles from Sarria to Portomarin. It will be a very leisurely walk when compared to many others to date. The weather is perfect, sunny and around sixty five with a nice breeze. The route today will also provide a nice mix of sun and shade.

I leave after breakfast at 10:00. I am in no hurry. I also need to stop at the Farmacia for sunblock. As I approach the Farmacia I pass a shop that can only be described as a junk shop. It carries everything from tee shirts to garden hoses. I will look in the shop for two items I need to complete the plan for my four Cross's.

The walk today starts out of the city by climbing fifty four steps to the Camino. Today I must also remember to begin having my Credential stamped at least twice a day. I am now within four days of Santiago. The one physical test for the day will come within the first two miles which is a long and fairly steep hill that fortunately is in the shade. I will complete the climb with three stops, I'm in no rush. Injury caused by foolish and aggressive tactics makes no sense. I am getting to close to risk that.

Along the way today I will see many new faces. They will be the new people who will walk from Sarria to Santiago, the shortest distance to walk and qualify for a Compostela.

Rainer leaves after having breakfast about an hour ahead of me. I will catch him later and we will walk the final three miles into Portomarin together. My pace today is very good but I need to be a bit more careful not to push it. Tomorrow I will be more cautious.

My four Cross's, what is the plan? First a little Camino history. For hundreds of years pilgrims would bring with them a stone with the name of someone on it that had passed away and leave it at a place they have selected on the Camino in memory of that person. Pilgrims would also bring a stone at the request of others. Rainer is carrying two such stones and will place them at a preselected location. I have been collecting seven stones along my Camino and I will place all seven at the monument at the top of the hill overlooking Santiago often called the monument of Happiness. It has this name because it will bring happiness to the pilgrim as he sees for the first time his destination, Santiago. I will tell you more about the stones shortly but first my four Cross's.

As I was training months ago I thought about the stones and how many I would bring and for whom. I also decided to do something else in addition to the stones. I would leave four Cross's buried on the Camino. I have sent to Robin a picture of my four Cross's all of which are silver and each a bit different while at the same time they are exactly alike. They are in a small metal box and include two notes, one which I will share with you, the other to be read only by the person, perhaps one of my grandchildren or another family member who finds the box. The box will be buried between Sarria and Santiago and I will record its exact location which will be sent to Robin along with pictures.

The part of the note I will share with you says:

> Hello,
>
> I am not sure who you are but congratulations on finding the box. I hope you are enjoying your Camino as much as I did mine. More importantly, I hope you are here as an act of gratitude for all of the gifts and blessings you have received just as I did in 2013.
>
> There are four Crosses in the box. Pin one to your backpack, it will keep you safe. Bring the other three home. Give one to Nanna, one to your Mother and give the last one to someone who is very special to you.
>
> Safe travels, and may God continue to bless you.
> Love Poppy.

I have not decided exactly where I will leave the box, I am working on that but it will be near a monument to be used as a reference point that will in all likelihood be here on the Camino for many years to come.

I will tell you about the stones tomorrow. Back to my walk to Portomarin.

This walk was uneventful, but almost a repeat of one of my past detours. As I am walking and thinking about how big a mistake it was not to think quickly enough to get a picture of the Dos Jose's, I realize that I can turn this lapse into something really great.

Robin has already begun planning a return trip to Spain next year which also includes a stop in Germany to have dinner with Michele and Rainer at Michele's restaurant in Dordmun. After Germany we will go to Spain and visit some of the cities where I did not get to see much because of the schedule I put myself on. While walking today I had what I think is a great idea.

We will include a visit to Villafranca, the village where the Dos Jose's brought me. We will stay at the Paradore and hire and English speaking driver to help us find the bar with the card games somewhere near a village called San Juan P something. Believe it or not I do know what direction it is from Villafranca and I know that it's about forty kilometers away. I doubt there are a lot of San Juan P something's.

We will go late in the afternoon, around 3:00 to 4:00, the same time I wandered into that parking lot. I hope to find one or both of the Jose's where I will have my picture taken with them and also get a picture of the Pink Panther car!

As I am walking along today completely focused on putting this idea together the two people I just passed on the Camino yell out to me. I turn around and they are waving at me because I just walked right past the left turn I was supposed to make to stay on the Camino. I almost took a "detour" thinking about how to put this idea together. Saved again by two strangers!

Rainer and I arrive at the hotel, its 4:25. My walk today took about six hours. It was a really good day. Now to get my gear taken care of, rest a bit and then two things. Dinner and then I open the card Amanda gave me with instructions not to do so until my 30th day, which is today.

I have only four days of walking ahead of me. Tomorrow will be Stage 31 a walk from Portomarin to Palas De Rei, fifteen and a half miles. I also will share with you the plan for the stones. Have a great day.

Sunday, June 16, 2013
Stage 31 a walk of fifteen miles to Palas De Rei…I wonder if David is still tired? Happy Fathers' Day!

I did not realize it was Father's Day until this morning when I received an email from Robin. So to all of the Fathers out there, Happy Father's Day. I wish I was there. I will be soon. I only have about 45 miles remaining and just three more days. It's hard to believe.

I did not sleep very well last night. A combination of a bed that just was not comfortable and a room that was a little too warm for me. I will get over it. I'm on my way to breakfast.

It's the usual, that's all I will say with one exception. Today the coffee is not very good. I will pass and just get something at my first stop, Gonzar, which is about five miles from my starting point.

The first two miles are where all of the days walking challenges will be. After the elevation change which is up about 900 feet, the Camino will be flat and in good condition. The weather is perfect, a little cloud cover, a slight breeze and plenty of shade make for what I think is the easiest day yet. Yes, I know fifteen miles is difficult but trust me fifteen in these conditions is much better than six on a difficult trail.

I am in the lobby trying to download email and send the Stage 30 post because the Wi-Fi only works in the lobby. As I am trying to get that accomplished I am sitting in the lobby looking at the map for today's walk. I am interested in trying to determine if there are any surprise turns or more than one trail. Yes, I know exactly what you are all saying right now…Jim's reading a map, this could be trouble.

You are correct. I have proven that I am not to be trusted with a map. It has given me a new found level of respect for the work being performed by that woman in the dashboard of my car.

That reminds me, I have a person in my iPad Mini who is starting to get under my skin. He or she was hired by Steve Jobs to guess what word I am trying to type. It bugs me. You know, you type in the first two letters of a word and he or she just takes a guess and slips in a word. This is annoying. I will admit that there are many occasions where the word is the same I am trying to type and that does help out.

I don't know who this person is in my Mini but I do know this. He or she never won a spelling bee. Speaking of spelling this reminds me of one of the best Management moments of my career. I'm sorry but when you are walking for more than six hours like I was today these things do pop into your head.

Here is what happened. It was the mid 80's and I was traveling constantly. I just returned to the office after a road trip and my assistant is filling me in on what I missed while I was gone. She says to me "we have a problem". Okay tell me what it is.

Jan tells me that David, a young man on the sales desk has developed a habit of calling in sick on Mondays when I am away and it's causing problems with phone coverage. Okay, I'll take care of it. I call David into my office and we have a conversation. That would be a BC Jim conversation where I do all of the talking and he just listens. I tell Jan our problem has been fixed.

About two or three weeks later I fly to the west coast on Sunday so I can be with customers on Monday morning. I call the next morning to see if I have any messages and Jan brings me up to speed and then says "David's not in today". You can't be serious.

I asked if he called in sick and so help me she says "no, he called in and said he was tired"! What I said next was an immediate response, immediate.

"Jan I want you to drop everything you have planned for today and find David, get him on the phone, tell him you spoke to me and then tell him Jim said, get a piece of paper and a pencil and write down the word TIRED and change the first letter to F"! Brilliant, simply brilliant. Come on, you have to agree that was pretty good.

Who said you can't have fun at work. I think Jan actually liked it more than I did. I wonder if David is still tired.

Back to the Camino. As I already said, it's a beautiful day. I am making such good time that I find myself telling me to slow down. There is absolutely no reason for going too fast. I left Portomarin at 10:00 and will arrive at 4:15, which includes stops where I have a bite to eat and give the passengers some airtime.

Say hello to Tilley the talker. I am on the Camino and all is good. I can hear her behind me. She is a good distance back but I can hear her like she is standing next to me. She never takes a breath! It's constant. I am not walking with her but I am on the verge of a headache. I cannot believe what the guy she is with must be going through. It's so bad that I decide to take a break and let them pass. They are not wearing backpacks or carrying anything so they should be faster. I stop and take off my backpack. She is talking non-stop all the way to me and for as far as I can see once they pass me. The Camino is quiet; she apparently did not get the memo. Tilley the Talker, that's the name I give her and I will see her again three more times today and each time she will be talking without interruption. This guy is either a saint or he is deaf.

The balance of my walk today in Stage 31 is uneventful. No detours. My walk today will be about six and a half hours.

Now, the Stones. I will have seven to be placed at the Mount Joy, Monte de Gozo, and a monument that commemorates the visit of Pope John Paul II from which the Cathedral towers can be seen. It will be that moment when I know that I have arrived in Santiago.

The seven stones. First, there will be one stone simply marked with "THE LIST". It represents all of those who I have on my "list" which dates back more than fifty years, started on the day my Grandfather died when I was about 15 years old. The list has grown as a list of this kind will. I have it memorized. This stone will be for all on the "list".

Each of those for whom I will place a single stone is also on the list. They are: My parents, my brother Bobby, my sister Susan, Robin's father and Clara, Bill's Mother. Beth understands the list and I know she will like the idea.

As I am walking along I am looking at individual stones which I think will represent all seven. Once I have selected and marked them I will send a photo to Robin to distribute among family. The picture of Clara's stone will be sent directly to Bill and Beth.

The markings on the stones won't last very long but the idea will last forever.

One last comment before I go. I opened Amanda's envelope and it was just the icing on the cake for what has been a really great day. With that I will say good night. Thanks for joining me, I will be there soon.

Tomorrow I walk to Ribadiso, a walk of 16 miles. Just three Stages remain. I'm close, really close. Good night.

Sunday, June 16, 2013
Stage 32...My walk today will be 17 miles to Arzua....

The tool I bought at the junk shop is no match for this hard rock soil. Rain, cold, wind and mud make for a very, very long day. I tested the tool I bought and it won't do the job. I need to find a real shovel or something close to it to dig an adequate hole for my four Cross's. The good news is that as I walked into this very small village I walked right past a hardware store. Yesterday was Sunday so it was closed. The hotel clerk thinks it will open today around 9:30. I guess they are not in a hurry to get their day started. By the way the picture of my Crosses is attached to the Stage 30 blog.

When I went to meet Rainer for dinner it was raining and getting cold. It's been raining all night and it appears that it will rain for all of my seventeen miles today. Not a problem, no complaints. I have had fantastic weather for all but a few tough days back at the beginning of my Camino, so this was somewhat overdue.

There is only one route and the trail will be mostly flat with an uphill portion starting around the ten mile point. The rain has been steady all night so it's likely that there will be mud. My poles are now veterans and will once again get me through it.

Breakfast is in the basement of the building. Its 7:30 but I can't leave until I get a chance to visit the hardware store which does not open until 9:30. There are no windows at breakfast so when I go back up the stairs to the lobby I am pleasantly surprised to see that not only has it stopped raining, it's also sunny and getting warmer. I think it's going to be a good day. I will be wrong.

When I woke this morning I could also sense a head cold getting started. I will plan on stopping at the Farmacia on my way out of the village. First stop the hardware store for the tool.

The clerk at the store does not understand me so I just begin looking around the store and I do find one tool which will work. It's a hand held version of a pickax. I buy it. The handle is detached from the head which will make packing it easy.

I am leaving the village and I stop at the Farmacia. My cold is getting worse and my throat's not all that good. The Farmacia is so small that four people waiting for help is going to take forever. I decide it can't wait. This was a bad decision.

The weather is cold but sunny. I can see the dark sky off in the distance and it appears that I am headed that way. The walk should be fairly flat. I will find out that with five miles to go I will be very, very wrong. The last five miles today will be straight up hill and will rain without stopping for all five miles.

After only one mile I am overheating and stop for a wardrobe change; I will repeat this routine four or five times in the first three hours. It's time consuming and it's not really resting in spite of the fact that you are not walking and your backpack is on the ground. This is really slowing me down and it's an energy burner.

I am about six miles from my starting point when it starts to rain. The trail s covered in mud and puddles which means there is no straight line to walk, every step is zigging and zagging around the mud and standing water. The poles are hard at work. Again an energy burner.

The rain is now steady and as I am doing the mud dance I am working on an idea for my four Cross's. I think I have the spot picked out. I will bury them today in the rain. One of the challenges I face in trying to close the book on my four Cross's idea is the pilgrim traffic. I would like to do this without a witness becoming curious. I really don't have a concern about someone doubling back to dig it up but I would feel better if I can do it privately. That won't be a problem because of the rain.

As it rains nonstop and I am working hard I am also sweating so much that I am getting wet from the inside out.

There is a beautiful little church in a small village of Santa Marie. It is near here that I have decided to bury my four Cross's. I find the spot, it's also symbolic and I dig the hole with my new tool and take pictures with both my iPhone and my iPad. I will send them to Robin and it will be quite easy to find the location which is very near a permanent structure which will be here for years to come.

I am so wet from the sweat and so worn out from all the stops that when it stops raining with about seven miles to go I take off my rain jacket and decide that if it rains again I will just get wet. Within a mile I am now just walking in the rain without the rain jacket. I will just get wet. I've done it before in the first few days at the start of my Camino, no big deal.

The last five miles are a real test made more difficult because I did not see it coming. I arrive at the hotel at 6:30 nearly eight and a half hours after I started. Because of the wardrobe delays, the Cross's burial and a couple of stops for food and coffee this day is not only somewhat difficult, it's also long.

I meet Rainer at 7:30 for dinner. Dinner is good but my cold is now becoming a serious issue. I feel like crap and when I speak you think you are talking to Barry White. Now my problem is I need to get to a Farmacia but none will open until 10:00 tomorrow morning. That's not good. Rainer asks the waiter what time the Farmacia opens and he does say 10:00 but wait, there is also a twenty four hour emergency Farmacia. It's about a mile and a half from where I am sitting. It's now about 9:00.

The last thing I am going to do is to walk another three miles trying to find a Farmacia in the dark while it's raining. I can't find the Camino In day light and perfect weather so trying to find a Farmacia on foot while it's raining in the dark is out of the question.

The waiter says he will try to get a taxi to come and take me. Ronald to the rescue. Ronald is the taxi driver who picks me up. He says to me in perfect English, "what do you need at the pharmacy"? I explain.

We arrive at the emergency Farmacia and it's just a tiny window that cannot be more the two feet square. Ronald gets out, rings the service button and he explains what is wrong with me and just like that the guy in the Farmacia puts my cold medicine in the push out delivery door. I am now given my LAFOR Polvo Para Solucion Oral and we are on our way back to the hotel. Ronald explains dosage and also says "no beer". A taxi driver and a Doctor.

I am ready to get to sleep. It's been a very long day. I now have only two more days of walking. Tomorrow I will walk to O Pedrouzo, Stage 33, 13 miles. I hope the LAFOR works!

Good night.

Tuesday, June 18, 2013
Stage 32...I am really close, I am as shocked as you are... Today 13 miles closer to the goal, Santiago

Fortunately the medicine is working. I feel much better today than when I went to bed last night. I guess walking in the cold rain was not good for me. I'm really close but I'm also really tired.

Breakfast is what it is, you just get used to it. I will get a head start on Rainer. He will be at a different hotel tonight because my hotel is sold out. We will meet for dinner on Wednesday in Santiago.

Unlike yesterday the weather this morning is clear but it's cold. It's 18 C or about 57 F. That's a good temperature for walking, but throw in some wind and it gets a little chilly. It's much better than yesterday and there is no point in dwelling on it. You just deal with it and go.

The Camino is crowded today. It feels like a "walkathon". With very few exceptions they are all new faces. I do see from time to time a few of the children, they are all spread out.

It's a nice day and the trail is much better. The mud for the most part is gone. No surprise hills, just 13 miles. I am moving at a pretty good pace because I keep passing people but I'm not pushing it. I don't take my first break until I've gone about five miles. A little something to eat, water and a snack and I am back on the Camino.

I think I am more focused because I am getting so close. I have all of the stones, they have all been marked and will be placed at The Hill of Happiness tomorrow just as I get set to enter the city. I will leave about the same time as I did today, 10:00. I could leave earlier to try and make the Pilgrims Mass at noon but that would just mean pushing it. I will attend the Pilgrims Mass on Thursday; it will be a lot easier. Getting my Compostela tomorrow will be my focus followed by buying one long sleeve shirt I can wear to dinner and then on the flight home. All of the clothes I came with will not be returning.

I arrive in O Pedrouzo at 3:30, five and a half hours. It's amazing how the trail conditions will effect time. It's also amazing how fast you can walk 13 miles when you know that it's going to bring you to the last Stage of this 500 mile journey!

Now a little dinner, some cold medicine and some sleep before I start Stage 34 a walk of only 12 miles to Santiago. Just think that for those of you on the west coast, I will be completing my Camino at the Cathedral of Saint James as you have your morning coffee, I hope you enjoy it as much I will enjoy seeing the Cathedral. Good night.

Tuesday, June 18, 2013
A post before the post....I made it! I am in Santiago and will soon post the Stage 34 blog.

Tuesday, June 18, 2013
Stage 34...It's the final Stage to Santiago. One million steps, five hundred miles and a great number of really incredible memories.

I will first have coffee con leche and then push off to Santiago. I have already started dumping anything I don't need to get to or stay in Santiago. I could leave my poles behind but I thought that they have really worked hard to help get me here and that the least I could do is let them walk into Santiago with me. We will part company before I leave on Friday morning for my connecting flight to Madrid.

It was a somewhat restless night due to a combination of my cold and a bit of anticipation; I just want to go and finish. I was asleep early and awake every couple of hours until I just gave up at 6:00. Each time I woke up I would look out the window to check the weather. It's been raining all night, not a heavy rain but a steady rain.

If this rain continues for my final Stage then it will be Barry White getting the Compostela at the Pilgrim Office. I was feeling a little better and thought that it might be Louie Armstrong instead. I will just have to deal with it one last time, continue to take the LAFOR and walk into Santiago with a cold.

I will not be getting to Santiago in time for the Pilgrims' Mass at noon anyway, so I will just wait and see if the weather changes. It is now

6:30; I will leave between 9:00 and 10:00. The Pilgrim's Office is open until 7:00 tonight. Rainer has already warned me that there will be a line which could mean that it may take an hour or more. I really don't care. I will just wait to see the swinging of the giant incense burner, Botafumeiro until tomorrow. The Cathedral seats up to 1000 people so there is a good chance that I will get a seat.

I finish breakfast at 8:15 and it does not look like it's going to be getting much better. I am leavening early and will just take my time on this my final walk to Santiago. I am so glad there isn't a Stage 35.

I pack my gear for the last time and exclude a couple of items like the detergent. I will not miss having to do that little sink task again. It is 9:30 as I return to the Camino. I will make several stops along the way for water, coffee and to have my Credential stamped at least three times.

The temperature is nearly perfect, about sixty degrees and just a slight breeze and it's cloudy. There are sections of the trail where there is mud but nothing that will cause me to perform the mud dance. The rain has left the trail soft which is good for the Limos and their passengers. I am dressed as well as I can given the fact that I don't have many options.

I have all seven stones in my backpack and they will be placed at The Hill of Happiness which will be about ten miles from my starting point. I will take several pictures today including a few of the markers which count down the number of kilometers remaining to Santiago. Each is a clear reminder of just how close I am.

It begins to rain after only two miles but I am in the forest so the tree cover acts as an umbrella making the rain a non-event. As I come out of the forest the rain stops and I will make my first wardrobe change. It's getting a little warm and of course I am heating up from inside the rain jacket.

With about four miles to go I make my final stop for coffee. It's a very small place and very few customers. As I drink my coffee it begins to rain. The two people who work here are completely glued to the television as they watch the American reality show filmed in a pawn shop in Detroit. The show is a less than flattering example of how people in the U.S. behave.

I reach Monte do Gozo which is now marked by the sizable monument commemorating the visit by Pope John Paul the second. The Hill of Happiness. It is certainly not the view that pilgrims from a thousand years ago had from the top of hill. It is very different I am sure. Hundreds of years ago the pilgrims could actually see the Cathedral from this location but now all you see is the outer edges of the suburbs of Santiago.

I place the seven stones at the base of the monument and take a few pictures. Robin will send them to family and others. This is my final task. I begin my walk downhill into Santiago. I walk past the Monte del Gozo Albergue which is within a couple hundred feet of the monument. It has beds for up to three thousand pilgrims! Can you imagine the sounds that three thousand people in bunk beds can make! It's actually a row of buildings which are filled with beds. I am so glad that Sharel didn't book me here!

As I walk over a freeway bridge I see it. It's the sign that simply says SANTIAGO. I take a picture, I have arrived, and my Camino walk is complete. I made it! Five hundred miles, one million steps.

The Camino Frances. It's a bit odd because I am walking alone and there isn't anyone to say "hey I made it", I have completed my Camino.

The next item on my agenda is to go to the Pilgrims office near the cathedral and claim my Compostela but first I want to find the hotel to shower and change. Everything I am wearing is wet and I don't want to stand in line as wet as I am still carrying all of my gear.

I get to my room and take a much needed shower. Rainer has just arrived and I will meet him in the lobby to leave for the Pilgrim's office. He's been there twice before so he knows the drill.

We get to the Pilgrims office and as luck would have it there is no line and I present my Credential's to the clerk. She inspects them. I have two now because the American version is too small. She asks me to complete a short questionnaire. She stamps my Credential's and hands them back to me along with my Compostela. The Compostela is in Latin and it includes my Latin name, Jacobum. Not exactly flattering is it?

Rainer and I will have dinner and then I will do my best to sleep in tomorrow morning. The only thing I have planned for Thursday is to attend the Pilgrims Mass at noon.

I will post my final blog as a summary of my Camino. I will write it on the plane back to Los Angeles on Friday, I'm taking Thursday off. That's it for now, no more walking, I am in Santiago.

See you soon. Good night.

Friday, June 21, 2013
My journey on the Camino....An attempt to summarize what is not possible to summarize.

It's all part of "the journey". That's what I have heard a friend say many times while we are playing golf. More specifically Bobby gets stuck with me as a partner and when I play poorly he would always say "it's all part of the journey". He is a very good player, I am not. As badly as I play he never gets upset…"it's all part of the journey". I have a new understanding of what that means to me after the Camino.

I did not mention this in the Stage 34 blog so I will now. As I was approaching the Hill of Happiness, I was met by a local TV crew, one reporter and a cameraman. They were from TV Galicia. It said so in big blue letters on the side of their small white car.

As I got closer to them the reporter started to move toward the trail, microphone in hand. I stopped and he asked me a question, first in Spanish and then after I responded in English he asked the question again. The question was basically how was it to walk in the rain? I responded "it's all part of the journey". He thanked me and I walked away with the camera man following me as I passed him. That's when it struck me that everything I have experienced on my 500 mile walk was in fact my journey and it had many parts to it. I doubt he understood my response and I don't think I'll be on the six o'clock news.

Rain, wind, snow, mud, cold, hot, blue skies and that's just the weather. Throw in the people, the difficulty, the discomfort, the fear of failure and so much more and you start to understand that it really is a journey. It's is a journey I will never forget.

I will also take from this journey new tools which I will use in my coaching business. I look forward to getting back to my work with a young and talented sales team.

My goal when I left California on May 13th was to complete the Camino. I can't describe the feeling of the fear of failure. I had worked hard to prepare but I did not have any idea of what I would be facing when I took my first step onto the Camino in St. Jean, France. Was I really ready? Could I walk ten or more days consecutively carrying more than twenty two pounds on my back? In the end I will walk thirty four days in a row without taking a day off. That was not planned for; it just turned out that way.

The first test came on day two in the snow. Have I prepared for snow? No. I live in San Juan Capistrano, we don't have snow. That was the first test of my commitment. I am here as an act of gratitude for all the gifts and blessings I have received. Would the gratitude be for just one day and 17 miles because the snow caused me to quit? If I am here also to leave something for my grandchildren about whom I was, what would quitting on day two say about me?

It's easy to quit. Always is, always will be. That is not the message I want them to get from my Camino. Being injured and unable to complete the journey is one thing, quitting because of weather is not an option. I can also tell you that the ability to reject quitting is made much easier when each day starts with a message from one of the people who want to see me complete the journey. It is a truly motivating reminder of why you cannot quit. There is no way to let all of these people down, you must continue. And let's not forget that in my backpack is a card that I am not supposed to open until my 30th day on the Camino. Should I just go home and open it at the club on the 30th day after quitting? Not going to happen.

I shared with you some of my fondest work related stories. There many more. I trust that in time when Brayden and Taylor are old enough to understand what message I am trying to send them, that they will see far more than just the story about young David and changing Tired to Fired. The message I hope they will come away with is that it is wrong to behave the way young David did—calling in sick when you are not and putting more work on others because you are just selfish. Realizing that the result was correct. My methods may have been a bit unconventional but they did work.

When I was working I had cards printed, the size of a business card which simply stated our Value Proposition. The card said only this:

> We tell the truth…We do the right thing…We never promise what we can't deliver.

How would young David's actions line up with these values? Everyone had the card, it was laminated and we encouraged everyone to keep it with them at all times. Simple and it works. That's the message.

So here I am on an airplane from Santiago to Madrid where I will connect to a nonstop flight to Los Angeles, 5628 miles away. The flight will take thirteen hours, not much more than Stage 27's walk which was only 18 miles. That puts some things about the Camino in perspective.

I had dinner last night with both Rainer and Michele. The food was good and it was a good way to end the Camino. Michele walked the last two days by combining two Stages in order to meet us for dinner here in Santiago.

Before dinner I head back to the central part of the city, it's a short walk to do some shopping. It's raining and I buy an umbrella for three Euros. I guess I am preparing for my return to a fear of rain. Actually I buy the umbrella because it's chilly and I don't need to have my cold get any worse. It's getting much better, I don't sound like Barry White any longer.

We have a forth for dinner. A guy who is from Italy Michele met back in Astorga. Interesting guy, played on three teams that won the Italian Super Bowl, as in American football. Big guy very fit. He rode a bike for his Camino and did it in twenty days. He builds custom motorcycles for a living.

The question comes up about would you walk the Camino again? For me the answer is very easy. No. Not because I didn't enjoy my Camino. I said No because I enjoyed it so much that there is no way I could duplicate it. If I were to do it again I know that I would be constantly comparing any second attempt with the first which would only mean disappointment. Now throw in the fact that I'm not getting any younger, I don't want to train that hard again and perhaps it's easy to understand my "No" answer.

How could I ever walk to Villafranca without thinking of my "detour" and the Dos Jose's or my exit from Astorga when I stop at the tiny little Camino church and find that my Credential is missing and in a panic return to the hotel to begin a search for it? There are others, a ride in a cop car in Los Arcos, Lilo, Anna, Bono, Irish Ann, Big Billy, Burgos Ray, the Children just to name a few.

My Camino experience was very special when I think of Nelly and Fernando but of course Michele and Rainer were the two people I spent lots of time with. I look forward to having dinner with them again next year at Michele's Restaurant. I'm guessing we just might get a good table.

So here I am waiting to board Iberia flight 6171. I am eager to get home and yes the beard will stay for perhaps a week but not any longer.

There are so many people to thank who helped make my Camino possible but there are also some who I want to say a special thanks to.

To Pat who planted the seed. I know that you will enjoy your Camino and that you will meet some very interesting people. Thank you.

To Sharel without whom I would not have been able to complete my Camino. Sharel worked very hard to keep me out of bunk beds and put up with all of my constant changes. Thank you.

Last but not least, Robin who from the moment I first spoke of the idea of walking the Camino never stopped or wavered in her support. She put up with all of my training schedules and was there when I would express doubts about being able to go five hundred miles. Thank you, I Love You and I look forward to seeing you at the airport. Remember I will be the old guy with the mostly white beard!

So that's it, my blog is complete. I have enjoyed trying to get it posted every day and I wait with great anticipation for my final grade. Thanks for joining me. I hope you got something from it, perhaps even a laugh or two.

Buen Camino and may you be as blessed as I am. Jim.

Saturday, February 15, 2014
After the Camino

I will not attempt to explain all of the reasons why I have decided to continue my Camino journey blog nearly six months after I returned from Santiago. A recent meetings with friends who followed my journey and offered great support without hesitation while also asking me to go back and write again has certainly had an impact on my decision.

Their support helped me take my first step onto The Camino every day for 34 days and for that I will always be appreciative.

I am as surprised as anyone with the number of times people ask me if I will continue to write on my Blog. It does occur more often than anyone would believe. It's equally surprising that there continues to be people reading the Blog every day. The feedback has now caused me to rethink the idea of continuing to write.

Robin and I recently visited with a great friend who is fighting a personal medical challenge. I was moved beyond explanation when she told me how much she enjoyed reading my posts each day while facing a very difficult daily medical procedure none of us should ever have to endure.

I was thrilled and a little embarrassed when she said that the daily posts helped her greatly as she dealt with treatment and the fear of what she was facing. She enthusiastically told me how much she looked forward to waking in the morning eager to catch up on my journey. I can only hope that whatever I now post can in some small way continue to help her in the fight against this awful disease.

I will soon reach out to her and arrange a long lunch to sit with her and to more personally share with her my Camino. We had very little time on this last visit and I look forward to seeing her soon.

While she and others have been nice enough to tell me how much they looked forward to reading about my Camino journey, I now realize that for a few my daily writings caused them to see me differently. Unfortunately I have even sensed a degree of discomfort with some when we are in the same company.

I'm not sure why but I believe that it has to do with the references to my Camino's spiritual experience.

It was never my intention to write anything which could be seen as trying to force or promote my beliefs. I also never intended to make anyone uncomfortable but I'm afraid that has happened. More about that in the future.

My writings have always been focused on having my Grandchildren get a glimpse of who I was, how I think and my beliefs. I'm not trying to recruit anyone or judge anyone who sees the world differently. It was for that reason I kept much of my thoughts to myself. I avoided every person and conversation on The Camino of a political nature because as I said during my journey I was not going to allow any such conversations to in anyway destroy the very positive experience I was having. Believe me if I had decided to allow my political beliefs into the Blog it would have destroyed the purpose of what I was trying to accomplish.

I will continue to abide by that rule in any additional writings.

I have now been back for six months and I have had an opportunity to reflect on my Camino. On occasion I look at the photos taken many of which were not posted and they have helped me to recall many memories which also were not posted. I will be working on going a bit more granular.

Again, the primary goal will be my attempt to leave behind a story written for my Grandchildren which also continues to give me a personal reward.

My next post (no schedule) will be about my return. Until then, thanks for joining me, Jim.

Saturday, February 15, 2014
My Camino withdrawal...How can you miss walking 15 miles a day?

The question is for most people silly. Miss walking 15 miles a day? Who has the time to walk for five or six hours every day? Not many of us. It's also true that if you do it every day you would need more than six hours. Weather, hills, fatigue and more all play into the daily walk of 15 or more miles.

I walked 14 miles today on my old training route without my backpack and the added 22 pounds and it was very different. Today the weather was perfect down along the beach to San Clemente. No hills, no weather to deal with and no weight.

I took along a small snack and a bottle of water. No need to be concerned about the water because I can just stop at any number of gas stations or convenience stores along the way and buy whatever I need. Not exactly like The Camino.

The biggest difference was the lack of solitude. Traffic, trains along the beach, people on bikes, construction crews and the occasional police car or ambulance with its lights blinking and sirens blaring just don't remind me of The Camino.

I miss the solitude. The long walks in a strange place with endless views all without any unnatural sounds is tough to reproduce.

I was with Robin last week with friends at a birthday party when I was asked what I missed most about the journey. It made me think and I now know what it is—it's the solitude. That rare commodity we all just don't focus on—the peace and quiet to just be alone to think and reflect. I miss that.

When I tried to answer the question it caused me to remember something I did on The Camino which I did not write in my daily post. Not sure why I did not include it. Perhaps I just didn't think much of it at the time but I do now.

I was walking alone, it was a beautiful day and the trail was flat and in good condition. I could see forever in all directions. I stopped in the middle of the trail and took off my backpack and sat on a rock on the side of the trail. I had a snack and drank some water but my focus was simply to just look around me for as far as I could see and focus on just how special this place was and that I was one of a relatively small number of people who had the opportunity to experience this. Completely quiet, not a soul in any direction, I was alone. But I was wrong.

Out of nowhere a young Spaniard walked up to me. He just seemed to suddenly be there. I had sat there for a short time and I had focused on just taking it all in and being alone so I somehow just never saw him behind me on the trail. He walked up to where I was and simply said "Hola, Buen Camino". I returned the favor.

He stopped, removed his backpack and sat on a nearby rock. He drank a little water and said to me just this..."beautiful". I just shook my head. He then took out his pack of Spanish size Marlboros and lit one. He then offered me one and I took it not wanting to offend him. We sat there smoking our little Marlboro's without saying another word.

He finished his Marlboro, put on his backpack and once again said "Buen Camino" and he left. I never saw him again. That's what I miss about The Camino. The solitude, the occasional surprise and the knowledge that once I put on my backpack again I would be one step closer to my next surprise. I can't find that walking 14 miles to and from San Clemente.

I'm not complaining about living here. There are a lot of people who would love to live here. Soon when winter wraps its cold arms around people back east there will be a lot more who might want to take a walk with me to San Clemente even if it's a bit noisy.

I know there is more to write. I just need to find the motivation.

Lightning Source UK Ltd.
Milton Keynes UK
UKHW041115271218
334619UK00001B/1/P

9 781512 726046